AMC 10 Practice Tests
Volume 1

AlphaStar Academy
Math Development Team

About AlphaStar Academy

AlphaStar Academy is an education company based in California. It offers extensive training programs for gifted students towards national and international Math and Science competitions such as American Mathematics Competitions, MATHCOUNTS, USA Math Olympiads, USA Computing Olympiads, and F=ma.

Students and teams from AlphaStar Academy performed extremely well in Mathematics competitions and olympiads, with countless students finishing in the top 10 and teams finishing in first place in competitions including Harvard-MIT Math Tournament, Princeton Math Competition, Stanford Math Tournament, Berkeley Math Tournament, and Caltech Harvey Mudd Math Competition. Dozens of AlphaStar Academy students got perfect scores in AMC 8/10/12 over the years and most of the MATHCOUNTS California team members in recent years were AlphaStar students. Moreover, every year between 2017 and 2020, at least one of the six-member USA IMO team were AlphaStar students/alumni.

Starting 2020, AlphaStar Academy has started offering all of its courses and programs online:

https://alphastar.academy/

About the Authors

This book contains four AMC 10 practice exams with new problems and insightful solutions.

Most of the problems and solutions were written by AlphaStar/A-Star faculty. More than 100 AlphaStar students took the tests in the last few years. The tests were recently revised using the data from their results by a team of AlphaStar Math Developers with the goal of aligning the tests in terms of difficulty and style with the AMC 10 exams of 2020's.

The authors and contributors participated and got excellent results in Math competitions and olympiads. In particular, in AMC 10/12, they had dozens of Distinguished Honor Roll Awards which are given to only the top 1% of participants and some of them even got perfect scores. Dr. Ali Gurel, AlphaStar Academy co-founder and Math Director, led the team and did the final editing.

We thank everyone involved in helping bringing this book to life which hopefully will help many students in their math journeys.

Contributors to writing problems and solutions:

Aaron Lin, Alex Song, Ali Gurel, Alper Halbutogullari, Anders Olsen, Ashwath Thirumalai, Brian Shimanuki, Edwin Peng, Evan Chen, Handong Wang, Jennifer Zhang, Jerry Wu, Kevin Chang, Mehmet Kaysi, Patrick Lin, Rachel Zhang, Richard Spence, Richard Yi, and Vishal Arul

Giving invaluable feedback, new insights, and improvements:

Alper Halbutogullari, Andrew Lin, Joey Heerens, Lazar Ilic, Mehmet Kaysi, Richard Spence

Math Development Team who wrote more problems, solutions, and edited the tests:

Aaron Chen, Ali Gurel, Alice Zhong, Andrew Chang, Andrew Wen, Aniketh Tummala, Hanna Chen, Jamin Xie, Jiakang Chen, Jieun Lim, Kelly Cui, Linus Tang, Michelle Wei, Olivia Xu, Robert Yang, Richard Spence, Stephen Xia, Steven Pan

To The Reader

The American Mathematics Contest 10 (AMC 10) is a 75-minute, 25-question, multiple choice test taken in the USA and many other countries by thousands of students in 10th grade and below. The questions on the AMC 10 are not straightforward and require a higher level of mathematical understanding to be solved, encouraging students to think beyond textbook problems and basic formulas.

Similar to any other contest, scoring well on the AMC 10 requires practice and determination. After initially attempting the test problems, you might feel that it is impossible to score high. However, it is very likely that you are just unaccustomed to solving these types of problems. With practice, you will build your skills and intuition and the AMC 10 will not seem like such a difficult task anymore, but rather another challenge to extend your mathematical knowledge.

We have put in our best efforts to create high quality practice tests and help improve your skills. In order to use the book most effectively, you should try to simulate an actual testing environment, attempting to solve each set within the time limit of 75 minutes. However, if you are at first unable to finish all the problems within the time limit, you are encouraged to continue working and attempt all the problems on the test. Gradually, you will find that you can solve problems faster with confidence in the accuracy of your answers.

You should also attempt to improve your problem solving ability by continuously reviewing problems that you have trouble with. Simply looking at the answer key is not enough. Attempting problems first will help you practice applying what you know, find where you struggle, and learn more effectively. Then, we encourage you to read and follow through the written solutions. We strove to make the solutions motivated and intuitive and added many alternate solutions to show that there are usually more than one way to solve difficult contest problems. All of these strategies will help you build your skills and solve more problems with ease.

Lastly, remember to believe in yourself! Don't be discouraged. Keep working and eventually your goals will be within reach. All of us started from the bottom, but we have built long experience, and many of us have succeeded exceptionally, achieving high scores and advancing to the AIME and beyond through tireless practice. We hope that you learn from our experience and the problems and solutions we have provided. We wish you success in preparing for the AMC 10 and future mathematical endeavors. Have fun problem solving!

Table of Contents

AMC 10 PRACTICE TESTS VOL 1

TEST-1

INSTRUCTIONS

1. This is a twenty-five question multiple choice test. Each question is followed by answers marked A, B, C, D and E. Only one of these is correct.

2. SCORING: You will receive 6 points for each correct answer, 1.5 points for each problem left unanswered, and 0 points for each incorrect answer.

3. Only scratch paper, graph paper, rulers, protractors, and erasers are allowed as aids. Calculators are NOT allowed. No problems on the test *require* the use of a calculator.

4. Figures are not necessarily drawn to scale.

5. You will have **75 minutes** to complete the test.

1. Alice goes to a store to buy tangerines. A tangerine costs 5 dollars, but the store has a special discount: "Buy three, get two free!" If she buys 22 tangerines using the discount, how many dollars will she pay?

   (A) 60   (B) 65   (C) 70   (D) 75   (E) 80

2. Eugene will pay income taxes based on his \$100,000 income this year. The tax rate is as follows: 10% for the first \$10,000, 20% for the next \$40,000, and 30% for any income earned after that. How much in income taxes will he pay?

   (A) \$20,000   (B) \$24,000   (C) \$27,000   (D) \$28,000   (E) \$30,000

3. A, B, C, and D lie on a line, in that order. If $AC = 2 \cdot AB$ and $BD = 3 \cdot CD$, what is $\dfrac{BC}{AD}$?

   (A) $\dfrac{1}{5}$ (B) $\dfrac{1}{4}$ (C) $\dfrac{1}{3}$ (D) $\dfrac{2}{5}$ (E) $\dfrac{2}{3}$

4. Hasan has scored 73, 78, 79, and 82 points in his four math exams so far. What should he average on his fifth and sixth exams to increase his overall average to 80 points?

   (A) 83   (B) 84   (C) 85   (D) 86   (E) 88

5. In a classroom, 17 students do not play soccer and 15 students do not play basketball. If 4 students play both sports and 6 students play neither sport, how many students are in the classroom?

   (A) 30   (B) 32   (C) 34   (D) 36   (E) 40

6. What is the 124th smallest positive integer that has no odd digits?

   (A) 866   (B) 868   (C) 886   (D) 888   (E) 2000

7. Rachel wanted to add two two-digit numbers but instead multiplied them. Her incorrect result was 3927. What should have been the correct result?

   (A) 112   **(B)** 116   **(C)** 120   **(D)** 124   **(E)** 128

8. One morning, Ashwath biked from home to school in 15 minutes. That afternoon, his return trip home took 3 minutes less because he biked 2 miles per hour faster. In total, how many miles did he bike during the day between home and school?

   (A) 2   **(B)** 3   **(C)** 4   **(D)** 6   **(E)** 8

9. Let $\{a \, b \, c\}$ denote the median of a, b, and c. For example, $\{1 \, 3 \, 2\} = 2$ and $\{3 \, 4 \, 3\} = 3$. For how many integers x is it true that $\{\{1 \, 2 \, x\} \, 4 \, \{0 \, 5 \, x\}\} = x$?

   (A) 2   **(B)** 3   **(C)** 4   **(D)** 5   **(E)** infinitely many

10. If the quadratic polynomial $x^2 + kx + 12$ has at least one positive integer root, how many possible integer values for k are there?

    (A) 0   **(B)** 1   **(C)** 2   **(D)** 3   **(E)** 4

11. Regular hexagon $ABCDEF$ has side length 1. What is the area of the set of points inside the hexagon that are within $\frac{\sqrt{3}}{4}$ away from least one of the sides?

    (A) $\dfrac{9}{8}$ **(B)** $6\sqrt{3} - 9$ **(C)** $\sqrt{3}$ **(D)** $\dfrac{9\sqrt{3}}{8}$ **(E)** $\dfrac{9}{4}$

12. Let a, b, c, d, e be the roots of the polynomial

$$x^5 - 4x^4 + 3x^3 - 2x^2 + 9x - 3.$$

What is the value of

$$(2a + 1)(2b + 1)(2c + 1)(2d + 1)(2e + 1)?$$

(A) -277 (B) -32 (C) -1 (D) 32 (E) 277

13. A square $ABCD$ has side length 1. Points K, L, M, and N are constructed inside the square so that KAB, LBC, MCD, and NDA are equilateral triangles. What is the area of quadrilateral $KLMN$?

(A) $2 - \sqrt{3}$ (B) $2\sqrt{3} - 3$ (C) $4 - 2\sqrt{3}$ (D) $\sqrt{3} - 1$ (E) $6 - 3\sqrt{3}$

14. Three couples seat themselves in a van containing two rows of three seats each. Both members of each couple wish to sit either next to each other in the same row, or with one member seated directly behind the other. In how many distinct ways can they seat themselves?

(A) 18   (B) 48   (C) 72   (D) 96   (E) 144

15. A rectangular 3×5 card is folded so that one set of diagonally opposite corners meet. What is the area of the new shape?

(A) 9.8   (B) 9.85   (C) 9.9   (D) 9.95   (E) 10

16. How many ordered pairs of integers (m, n) are there such that $1 \leq m \leq 100$, $1 \leq n \leq 100$, and $m^n \cdot n^m$ leaves a remainder of 1 when divided by 4?

(A) 625   (B) 1250   (C) 2500   (D) 5000   (E) 7500

17. Richard rolls a fair six-sided die four times and records his rolls as a four-digit number. For example, if he rolls 1, 3, 3, 6, then he writes the number "1336." What is the probability that, if he rolls the die four times, the corresponding 4-digit number is divisible by 7?

(A) $\dfrac{185}{1296}$ (B) $\dfrac{1}{7}$ (C) $\dfrac{31}{216}$ (D) $\dfrac{187}{1296}$ (E) $\dfrac{1}{6}$

18. Linus wants to call his friend for exactly 29 minutes. An unusual phone company charges $n^2 - n + 5$ cents for an n-minute call, for all positive integers n. What is the least number of cents that Linus must pay the phone company for a series of phone calls summing to 29 minutes, assuming that each call takes a whole number of minutes?

(A) 101   (B) 102   (C) 103   (D) 104   (E) 105

19. An ant wishes to travel from A to B in the following 4×3 grid. Every second, the ant travels either 1 unit up or 1 unit right, and it will never move three or more consecutive units in the same direction. How many possible paths can the ant take from A to B?

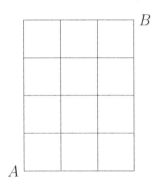

(A) 16   (B) 18   (C) 20   (D) 21   (E) 22

20. Let n be a positive integer. An integer is randomly chosen from 1 to 2^n inclusive. The probability that it has exactly 6 zeros in its binary representation is $\frac{1989}{16384}$. What is n?

(A) 14   (B) 15   (C) 16   (D) 17   (E) 18

21. Four boys and four girls each pick their favorite song from an album consisting of four songs. It was noted that no song was picked by both a boy and a girl. In how many different ways could they have picked their favorite songs?

    (A) 1416   **(B)** 1584   **(C)** 1668   **(D)** 1740   **(E)** 1812

22. Triangle ABC with sides 25, 39 and 40 is given. The angle bisectors of $\triangle ABC$ divide the triangle into six smaller triangles. What is the area of the smallest of these six triangles?

    (A) $\dfrac{4375}{158}$ **(B)** $\dfrac{8775}{158}$ **(C)** $\dfrac{7575}{128}$ **(D)** $\dfrac{1755}{26}$ **(E)** $\dfrac{1125}{16}$

23. For positive real number r, the inequality $a^3 + 4b^3 + 3 \geq r(a+b)$ is true for all positive real numbers a and b. What is the largest possible value of r?

    (A) $\sqrt{6}$ **(B)** $\sqrt{8}$ **(C)** 3   **(D)** $2\sqrt[3]{4}$ **(E)** 4

24. Two ants begin at opposite vertices of a cube with side length 1 meter and walk along the edges at 1 meter per second. At each vertex, each ant randomly picks an adjacent edge to transverse (which can be the edge it just came from). What is the expected value of the time, in seconds, it will take them to meet?

    (A) 11   **(B)** 11.5   **(C)** 12   **(D)** 12.5   **(E)** 13

25. Define $G_k = 2F_{k+1} - F_k$, where $\{F_k\}$ is the Fibonacci sequence given by $F_0 = 0$, $F_1 = 1$, and $F_k = F_{k-1} + F_{k-2}$ for all $k \geq 2$. If

    $$G_1 + G_2 + G_3 + \ldots + G_{2021} = F_a + F_b - F_c$$

    for some positive integers $a > b > c$, what is $a + b + c$?

    (A) 4049   **(B)** 4050   **(C)** 4051   **(D)** 4052   **(E)** 4053

Test-1 Answer Key

1. C
2. B
3. D
4. B
5. A
6. D
7. E
8. C
9. C
10. D
11. D
12. E
13. A
14. E
15. C
16. B
17. C
18. B
19. B
20. E
21. E
22. B
23. C
24. E
25. B

Test-1 Solutions

1. Alice goes to a store to buy tangerines. A tangerine costs 5 dollars, but the store has a special discount: "Buy three, get two free!" If she buys 22 tangerines using the discount, how many dollars will she pay?

(A) 60   **(B)** 65   **(C)** 70   **(D)** 75   **(E)** 80

Answer (C): The discount is equivalent to buying 5 for the price of 3. Using the discount, Alice can buy 4 sets of 5 tangerines for the price of 4 sets of 3 tangerines, for $4 \cdot 3 \cdot 5 = 60$ dollars, and then two more tangerines at 5 dollars each, totaling 70 dollars.

2. Eugene will pay income taxes based on his \$100,000 income this year. The tax rate is as follows: 10% for the first \$10,000, 20% for the next \$40,000, and 30% for any income earned after that. How much in income taxes will he pay?

(A) \$20,000   **(B)** \$24,000   **(C)** \$27,000   **(D)** \$28,000   **(E)** \$30,000

Answer (B): For the first \$10,000 of income, he pays \$1,000. For the next \$40,000, he pays \$8,000. For the last \$50,000, he pays \$15,000. Summing it up, he pays \$24,000.

3. A, B, C, and D lie on a line, in that order. If $AC = 2 \cdot AB$ and $BD = 3 \cdot CD$, what is $\dfrac{BC}{AD}$?

(A) $\dfrac{1}{5}$ **(B)** $\dfrac{1}{4}$ **(C)** $\dfrac{1}{3}$ **(D)** $\dfrac{2}{5}$ **(E)** $\dfrac{2}{3}$

Answer (D): $AC = 2 \cdot AB$ gives $AB = BC$. Also, $BD = 3 \cdot CD$ implies that $BC + CD = 3 \cdot CD$, so $BC = 2 \cdot CD$. Let $CD = a$. Then, $AB = BC = 2a$ and

11

$AD = 2a + 2a + a = 5a$. Finally,

$$\frac{BC}{AD} = \frac{2a}{5a} = \frac{2}{5}.$$

4. Hasan has scored 73, 78, 79, and 82 points in his four math exams so far. What should he average on his fifth and sixth exams to increase his overall average to 80 points?

   (A) 83 **(B)** 84 **(C)** 85 **(D)** 86 **(E)** 88

   Answer (B): The sum of his scores should be $80 \times 6 = 480$. So far, he scored

   $$73 + 78 + 79 + 82 = 312.$$

   Therefore, he needs to score a sum of $480 - 312 = 168$ on his last two exams, or an average of $\frac{168}{2} = 84$.

   Alternate Solution: His scores relative to 80 are $-7, -2, -1$ and $+2$ so far. Their sum is -8, so the sum of his next two scores should be $+8$ relative to 80, which means their average is $+4$ relative or 80, or 84.

5. In a classroom, 17 students do not play soccer and 15 students do not play basketball. If 4 students play both sports and 6 students play neither sport, how many students are in the classroom?

   (A) 30 **(B)** 32 **(C)** 34 **(D)** 36 **(E)** 40

   Answer (A): The students in the class can be split into two non-overlapping categories: those that play both sports and those that play at most one sport. The number of students that play both sports is given as 4. The number of students that play at most one sport, using the Principle of Inclusion and Exclusion, is $17 + 15 - 6 = 26$. The 6 students who play neither do not play soccer or basketball so they are counted in both 17 and 15 when counting the total. That is why we subtracted them. Thus, there are a total of $4 + 26 = 30$ students in the classroom.

   Alternate Solution: Among the 17 students who do not play soccer 6 of them do not play basketball either. Hence, the remaining $17 - 6 = 11$ students play only basketball. Similarly, $15 - 6 = 9$ students play only soccer. There are $11 + 9 = 20$ students playing only one sport. Adding this to the number of students who do not play either sport and those who play both sports, we find that there are $20 + 6 + 4 = 30$ students in the classroom.

6. What is the 124th smallest positive integer that has no odd digits?

   (A) 866 **(B)** 868 **(C)** 886 **(D)** 888 **(E)** 2000

   Answer (D): Let a_n be the nth smallest positive integer with no odd digits. Since there are 5 possibilities for each non-leading digit and 4 for the leading digit, a_n is just the base-10 number formed by doubling the digits of n's base-5 representation. Since $124 = 444_5$, $a_{124} = 888$.

7. Rachel wanted to add two two-digit numbers but instead multiplied them. Her incorrect result was 3927. What should have been the correct result?

   (A) 112 **(B)** 116 **(C)** 120 **(D)** 124 **(E)** 128

   Answer (E): We factor the given number as $3 \times 7 \times 11 \times 17$. The only way to write this as a product of two two-digit numbers is 51×77. So, the correct result would be $51 + 77 = 128$.

8. One morning, Ashwath biked from home to school in 15 minutes. That afternoon, his return trip home took 3 minutes less because he biked 2 miles per hour faster. In total, how many miles did he bike during the day between home and school?

   (A) 2 **(B)** 3 **(C)** 4 **(D)** 6 **(E)** 8

   Answer (C): Let his speed be v and $v + 2$ miles per hour, respectively. Then, we have $15v = 12(v + 2)$, giving $v = 8$ miles per hour. Therefore, in 15 minutes he bikes 2 miles. In total, he bikes $2 + 2 = 4$ miles.

9. Let $\{a\, b\, c\}$ denote the median of a, b, and c. For example, $\{1\, 3\, 2\} = 2$ and $\{3\, 4\, 3\} = 3$. For how many integers x is it true that $\{\{1\, 2\, x\}\, 4\, \{0\, 5\, x\}\} = x$?

(A) 2   **(B)** 3   **(C)** 4   **(D)** 5   **(E)** infinitely many

Answer (C): Note that if $x \geq 5$, then $\{1\,2\,x\} = 2$, $\{0\,5\,x\} = 5$, and $\{\{1\,2\,x\}\,4\,\{0\,5\,x\}\} = \{2\,4\,5\} = 4 \neq x$. Similarly, if $x \leq 0$, then $\{1\,2\,x\} = 1$, $\{0\,5\,x\} = 0$, and $\{\{1\,2\,x\}\,4\,\{0\,5\,x\}\} = \{1\,4\,0\} = 1 \neq x$. Hence we only need to check $x = 1, \ldots, 4$.

When $x = 1$, $\{1\,2\,x\} = 1$, $\{0\,5\,x\} = 1$, and $\{\{1\,2\,x\}\,4\,\{0\,5\,x\}\} = \{1\,4\,1\} = 1 = x$. So, $x = 1$ is a solution.

When $x = 2$, $\{1\,2\,x\} = 2$, $\{0\,5\,x\} = 2$, and $\{\{1\,2\,x\}\,4\,\{0\,5\,x\}\} = \{2\,4\,2\} = 2 = x$. So, $x = 2$ is a solution.

When $x = 3$, $\{1\,2\,x\} = 2$, $\{0\,5\,x\} = 3$, and $\{\{1\,2\,x\}\,4\,\{0\,5\,x\}\} = \{2\,4\,3\} = 3 = x$. So, $x = 3$ is a solution.

When $x = 4$, $\{1\,2\,x\} = 2$, $\{0\,5\,x\} = 4$, and $\{\{1\,2\,x\}\,4\,\{0\,5\,x\}\} = \{2\,4\,4\} = 4 = x$. So, $x = 4$ is a solution.

1, 2, 3, and 4 are all solutions.

Thus, there are a total of 4 integer solutions.

10. If the quadratic polynomial $x^2 + kx + 12$ has at least one positive integer root, how many possible integer values for k are there?

(A) 0   **(B)** 1   **(C)** 2   **(D)** 3   **(E)** 4

Answer (D): The sum and product of the roots are $-k$ and 12, respectively by Vieta's formulas. If one of the roots is a positive integer, then the second one must be positive as well because their product is 12, which is positive. The second root must also be an integer because their sum is $-k$, which is an integer. We conclude that the second root is a positive integer as well. So 12 is the product of two roots which are both positive integers, and $-k$ is their sum. We can write 12 as a product of two positive integers in three ways: $3 \cdot 4$, $2 \cdot 6$, and $1 \cdot 12$. These give us 3 possible values for k: -7, -8, and -13.

11. Regular hexagon $ABCDEF$ has side length 1. What is the area of the set of points inside the hexagon that are within $\frac{\sqrt{3}}{4}$ away from least one of the sides?

(A) $\dfrac{9}{8}$ **(B)** $6\sqrt{3} - 9$ **(C)** $\sqrt{3}$ **(D)** $\dfrac{9\sqrt{3}}{8}$ **(E)** $\dfrac{9}{4}$

Answer (D):

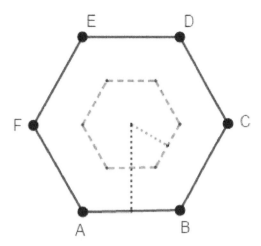

Let us draw the line segments inside the hexagon that are $\frac{\sqrt{3}}{4}$ away from the sides of the hexagon. They intersect to form a smaller regular hexagon as shown in the diagram. We notice that the set of points not satisfying the condition is the region inside this smaller hexagon, with radial height $\frac{\sqrt{3}}{4}$ less than that of the original hexagon. The radial heights are shown in the diagram by the dotted lines that are perpendicular to the corresponding sides of the hexagons. $ABCDEF$ has radial height $\frac{\sqrt{3}}{2}$, so the smaller hexagon has radial height $\frac{\sqrt{3}}{4}$, meaning the area of the smaller hexagon is a quarter of that of the original hexagon. So the area of the points satisfying the condition is $\frac{3}{4}$ of the area of the original hexagon. Hence, the desired answer is

$$\frac{3}{4} \cdot \frac{1^2 \sqrt{3}}{4} \cdot 6 = \frac{9\sqrt{3}}{8}.$$

12. Let a, b, c, d, e be the roots of the polynomial

$$x^5 - 4x^4 + 3x^3 - 2x^2 + 9x - 3.$$

What is the value of

$$(2a + 1)(2b + 1)(2c + 1)(2d + 1)(2e + 1)?$$

(A) -277 **(B)** -32 **(C)** -1 **(D)** 32 **(E)** 277

Answer (E): Let $P(x)$ be the given polynomial. Then,

$$P(x) = (x - a)(x - b)(x - c)(x - d)(x - e).$$

To use this factorization, we can rewrite $(2a+1)(2b+1)(2c+1)(2d+1)(2e+1)$ as

$$(-2)^5\left(-\frac{1}{2}-a\right)\left(-\frac{1}{2}-b\right)\left(-\frac{1}{2}-c\right)\left(-\frac{1}{2}-d\right)\left(-\frac{1}{2}-e\right) = -32P\left(-\frac{1}{2}\right).$$

We then compute $P\left(-\frac{1}{2}\right)$ simply by substituting $x=-\frac{1}{2}$ in the original polynomial:

$$P\left(-\frac{1}{2}\right) = -\frac{1}{32}-\frac{4}{16}-\frac{3}{8}-\frac{2}{4}-\frac{9}{2}-3 = -\frac{277}{32}.$$

Hence, the answer is $-32P\left(-\frac{1}{2}\right) = 277.$

13. A square $ABCD$ has side length 1. Points K, L, M, and N are constructed inside the square so that KAB, LBC, MCD, and NDA are equilateral triangles. What is the area of quadrilateral $KLMN$?

(A) $2-\sqrt{3}$ (B) $2\sqrt{3}-3$ (C) $4-2\sqrt{3}$ (D) $\sqrt{3}-1$ (E) $6-3\sqrt{3}$

Answer (A):

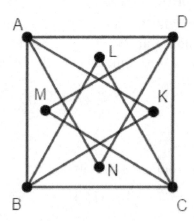

First note that, by symmetry, $KLMN$ is a square. Let $h=\frac{\sqrt{3}}{2}$ be the height of the equilateral triangles. Then, the distances from L to AD and N to BC are both $1-h$, so $LN = 1-(1-h)-(1-h) = 2h-1 = \sqrt{3}-1$.

Finally, the area of square $KLMN$ is $\dfrac{LN^2}{2} = 2-\sqrt{3}.$

14. Three couples seat themselves in a van containing two rows of three seats each. Both members of each couple wish to sit either next to each other in the same row, or with one member seated directly behind the other. In how many distinct ways can they seat themselves?

    (A) 18   **(B)** 48   **(C)** 72   **(D)** 96   **(E)** 144

    Answer (E):

A_1	A_2	A_3
B_1	B_2	B_3

Let A_1, A_2, A_3 and B_1, B_2, B_3 be the three seats from left to right in the front and back, respectively. There are three possible cases:

Case 1: Each couple has one partner in the front row and the other directly behind, in the second row: $A_1 - B_1$, $A_2 - B_2$, $A_3 - B_3$.

Case 2: One couple sits in the rightmost seats of each row. The second and third couples sit together on the remaining seats of the first and second rows, respectively: $A_1 - A_2$, $B_1 - B_2$, $A_3 - B_3$.

Case 3: The reflection of Case 2 along the center seats: $A_1 - B_1$, $A_2 - A_3$, $B_2 - B_3$.

For each case, there are 3! ways to assign the couples to the pairs of seats. There are 2 ways to order the people within each couple. The total number of arrangements is $3 \cdot 3! \cdot 2^3 = 144$.

Remark. Note that the number of cases above is $T_3 = 3$ where T_n is the number of ways of tiling a $2 \times n$ floor using 1×2 pieces. Observing the recurrence relation for T_n (i.e. $T_n = T_{n-1} + T_{n-2}$) and finding the first few terms $T_1 = 1$ and $T_2 = 2$, we find that T_n is the $(n+1)$st term of the Fibonacci sequence.

15. A rectangular 3×5 card is folded so that one set of diagonally opposite corners meet. What is the area of the new shape?

    (A) 9.8   **(B)** 9.85   **(C)** 9.9   **(D)** 9.95   **(E)** 10

    Answer (C):

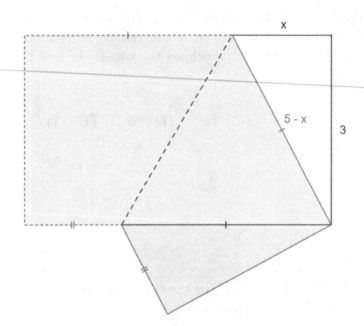

The new shape is a pentagon triangulated into two right triangles and an isosceles triangle. If the unknown leg of the right triangles has length x, the bases have lengths 3 and x and the hypotenuse has length $5 - x$. We have $3^2 + x^2 = (5 - x)^2$, so $x = 1.6$. Each of the triangles has area $\frac{3 \times 1.6}{2} = 2.4$. Since the original card consisted of the two triangles and twice the area of the isosceles triangle, the area of the isosceles triangle is $\frac{3 \times 5 - 2 \times 2.4}{2} = 5.1$. The area of the pentagon is $5.1 + 2 \times 2.4 = 9.9$.

16. How many ordered pairs of integers (m, n) are there such that $1 \leq m \leq 100$, $1 \leq n \leq 100$, and $m^n \cdot n^m$ leaves a remainder of 1 when divided by 4?

(A) 625   (B) 1250   (C) 2500   (D) 5000   (E) 7500

Answer (B): If $m^n \cdot n^m \equiv 1 \pmod 4$, then either $m^n \equiv n^m \equiv 1$ or $m^n \equiv n^m \equiv 3$ (mod 4).

For odd numbers a and b, $a^b \equiv a \pmod 4$ because $a^2 \equiv 1 \pmod 4$. Since m and n must be odd, the two cases above lead to: $m \equiv n \equiv 1$ or $m \equiv n \equiv 3$ (mod 4). Each of these give $25 \cdot 25 = 625$ pairs, so in total we have 1250 solutions.

17. Richard rolls a fair six-sided die four times and records his rolls as a four-digit number. For example, if he rolls 1, 3, 3, 6, then he writes the number "1336." What is the

probability that, if he rolls the die four times, the corresponding 4-digit number is divisible by 7?

(A) $\dfrac{185}{1296}$ (B) $\dfrac{1}{7}$ (C) $\dfrac{31}{216}$ (D) $\dfrac{187}{1296}$ (E) $\dfrac{1}{6}$

Answer (C): For $n \geq 1$, let p_n denote the probability that the n-digit number obtained from his first n rolls is divisible by 7. The problem is asking for p_4. Note that $p_1 = 0$ since none of the numbers $1, \ldots, 6$ is divisible by 7. Notice that if the first n rolls form a multiple of 7, the $(n+1)^{\text{th}}$ roll must form a number which is not a multiple of 7. On the other hand, if the first n rolls form a number which is not a multiple of 7, there is a $\frac{1}{6}$ probability that the next roll forms a multiple of 7. Thus, we have the recurrence

$$p_{n+1} = \frac{1}{6}(1 - p_n)$$

with $p_1 = 0$. We obtain $p_2 = \frac{1}{6}$, $p_3 = \frac{5}{36}$, and $p_4 = \frac{31}{216}$.

18. Linus wants to call his friend for exactly 29 minutes. An unusual phone company charges $n^2 - n + 5$ cents for an n-minute call, for all positive integers n. What is the least number of cents that Linus must pay the phone company for a series of phone calls summing to 29 minutes, assuming that each call takes a whole number of minutes?

(A) 101 (B) 102 (C) 103 (D) 104 (E) 105

Answer (B): Let $f(n) = n^2 - n + 5$. To find the best option, we consider the call rates $\frac{f(n)}{n}$. We find that $\frac{f(1)}{1} = \frac{5}{1}$, $\frac{f(2)}{2} = \frac{7}{2}$, $\frac{f(3)}{3} = \frac{11}{3}$, and $\frac{f(n)}{n} > 4$ for $n \geq 4$. The best rate is a 2-minute call with 3.5 cents per minute. Thus, he uses most of his call time with 2-minute calls. At the end, he can use a 1-minute call or a 3-minute call. Note that a 3-minute call is cheaper than three 1-minute calls and also cheaper than a 1-minute and a 2-minute call combined. Hence, the most efficient distribution of time is $29 = 13 \cdot 2 + 1 \cdot 3$ and it costs $13 \cdot 7 + 1 \cdot 11 = 102$ cents.

19. An ant wishes to travel from A to B in the following 4×3 grid. Every second, the ant travels either 1 unit up or 1 unit right, and it will never move three or more consecutive units in the same direction. How many possible paths can the ant take from A to B?

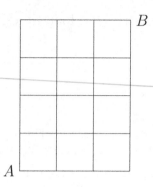

(A) 16   (B) 18   (C) 20   (D) 21   (E) 22

Answer (B): There are $\binom{7}{3} = 35$ shortest paths. We'll use complementary counting and subtract the ones that do not work. Let X and Y denote a step in the horizontal and vertical direction, respectively. We can thus represent each path as a sequence of four Y's and three X's, but to use complementary counting, we want the ones that contain XXX and/or YYY.

Case 1: YYY appears but $YYYY$ doesn't appear in the sequence.
There are 4 ways to choose the position of YYY relative to the three X's and then 3 remaining ways to choose the position of the fourth Y, which cannot be adjacent to YYY. So this gives $4 \cdot 3 = 12$ paths.

Case 2: $YYYY$ appears.
There are 4 ways to choose the position of $YYYY$.

Case 3: XXX appears but YYY doesn't appear.
There is only 1 such path which is $YYXXXYY$.

In total, there are $12 + 4 + 1 = 17$ non-desired paths and $35 - 17 = 18$ desired ones.

Alternate Solution: We use case work based on the sizes of chunks of Y's. For example $XYYXYXY$ has Y groups with sizes 2, 1, 1. For any valid path, the four Y's must be split into groups of 1's and 2's. The cases up to order are $(1, 1, 1, 1)$, $(1, 1, 2)$, and $(2, 2)$.

Case 1: $(1, 1, 1, 1)$. There is only 1 case: $YXYXYXY$.

Case 2: $(1, 1, 2)$. We must have $YXYXYY$ and one more X. Depending on where the last X goes, this leads to 4 possibilities: $XYXYXYY$, $YXXYXYY$, $YXYXXYY$, and $YXYXYYX$. Each of these have 3 ways for permuting their Y groups (the double Y can be the first, second, or last group), so this gives $4 \cdot 3 = 12$ cases.

Case 3: $(2, 2)$. We must have $YYXYY$ and two more X's. There are 3 spots where the two X's can go. Using stars and bars, we get $\binom{3+2-1}{3-1} = \binom{4}{2} = 6$ cases. However, note that the two X's cannot both end up in the middle group (or it would lead to a block of three X's). Thus, we have $6 - 1 = 5$ cases.

Overall, there are $1 + 12 + 5 = 18$ such paths.

20. Let n be a positive integer. An integer is randomly chosen from 1 to 2^n inclusive. The probability that it has exactly 6 zeros in its binary representation is $\frac{1989}{16384}$. What is n?

(A) 14   **(B)** 15   **(C)** 16   **(D)** 17   **(E)** 18

Answer (E): For $n \geq 7$, we claim that the number of integers from 1 up to 2^n that have exactly 6 zeros in its binary representation is $\binom{n}{7}$. To see this, first note that for $n \geq 7$, the number 2^n does not work as it has n zeros which is more than 6. We can think of positive integers less than 2^n as having n places where one of these places is selected as the leading 1 and the places to the right are each assigned a 0 or 1. The desired numbers have 6 other special places to the right of the leading 1, for the 6 zeros. So if we select 7 places among the n places, the leftmost one for the leading 1 and the remaining 6 places for the six 0's, this selection uniquely determines the desired number.

For example, when $n = 10$, the number

$$110000001_2$$

would be determined by the selection

$$\star S \star SSSSSS\star$$

where among the 10 places, the 7 S's show the 7 selected places and the 3 stars show the non-selected places.

Hence, there are indeed $\binom{n}{7}$ such numbers.

We want

$$\frac{\binom{n}{7}}{2^n} = \frac{1989}{16384}.$$

By looking at the denominator, we notice that $16384 = 2^{14}$, so

$$\binom{n}{7} = 1989 \times 2^{n-14} = 9 \times 13 \times 17 \times 2^{n-14}.$$

Since this is a multiple of 17, $n \geq 17$. Checking $n = 17$ we see that $\binom{17}{7}$ is not a multiple of 9 so it doesn't work. However, $n = 18$ works since

$$\binom{18}{7} = 9 \times 13 \times 17 \times 16 = 1989 \times 2^{18-14}.$$

So $n = 18$.

21. Four boys and four girls each pick their favorite song from an album consisting of four songs. It was noted that no song was picked by both a boy and a girl. In how many different ways could they have picked their favorite songs?

(A) 1416   **(B)** 1584   **(C)** 1668   **(D)** 1740   **(E)** 1812

Answer (E): We do casework on B, the number of distinct songs picked by the boys.

Case 1: $B = 1$. There are 4 ways to pick this song, and then $3^4 = 81$ ways for the girls to pick from the remaining songs, giving $4 \cdot 81 = 324$ ways.

Case 2: $B = 2$. There are two sub-cases here:

If three boys pick one song and the last boy picks a second song, there are $4 \cdot 3 \cdot \binom{4}{1} = 48$ ways for the boys to pick songs.

If two boys pick one song and the other two boys pick another song, there are $\binom{4}{2}$ ways to pick two songs, and $\binom{4}{2}$ ways to decide which boys pick the first song, giving $\binom{4}{2}^2 = 36$ ways for the boys to pick songs.

Then there are $48 + 36 = 84$ ways for the boys to pick songs under these constraints, and the girls can pick songs in $2^4 = 16$ ways, since each girl can pick from one of two remaining songs, giving $84 \cdot 16 = 1344$ ways.

Case 3: $B = 3$. Two of the boys must select the same song in this case. There are 4 ways to select the song picked by these two boys, $\binom{4}{2}$ ways to pick the two boys that pick this song, then $3 \cdot 2$ ways for the remaining boys to select two distinct songs. This gives $4 \cdot \binom{4}{2} \cdot 3 \cdot 2 = 144$ ways.

Altogether, the number of ways is $324 + 1344 + 144 = 1812$.

22. Triangle ABC with sides 25, 39 and 40 is given. The angle bisectors of $\triangle ABC$ divide the triangle into six smaller triangles. What is the area of the smallest of these six

triangles?

(A) $\dfrac{4375}{158}$ **(B)** $\dfrac{8775}{158}$ **(C)** $\dfrac{7575}{128}$ **(D)** $\dfrac{1755}{26}$ **(E)** $\dfrac{1125}{16}$

Answer (B):

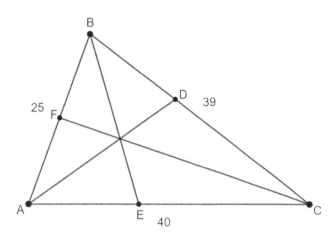

Notice that all six triangles have the same height of length r, the inradius. Therefore, to find the smallest area we need to find the smallest base.

Without loss of generality, let $AB = 25$, $BC = 39$ and $AC = 40$. Let the angle bisectors of the angles A, B and C intersect the sides BC, AC, and AB at D, E, and F, respectively. Using the Angle Bisector Theorem we see that $BD < DC$, $AE < EC$, and $BF < AF$. Moreover we can calculate these bases in terms of the side lengths using the angle bisector theorem.

$$\frac{BD}{BC} = \frac{25}{65} \ \Rightarrow \ BD = \frac{39 \cdot 25}{65} = 15.$$

Similarly, we find

$$AE = \frac{40 \cdot 25}{64} = \frac{125}{8} \quad \text{and} \quad BF = \frac{25 \cdot 39}{79} = \frac{975}{79}.$$

Note that BF is the smallest of the six segments.

To find the inradius, we use the formula $[ABC] = s \cdot r$, where $s = \frac{25+39+40}{2} = 52$ is the half-perimeter. Area of $\triangle ABC$ can be calculated by dropping the altitude from A and dividing the triangle into two right triangles with sides 7-24-25 and 32-24-40. So

$$\frac{39 \cdot 24}{2} = 52r \ \Rightarrow \ r = 9.$$

Finally,

$$[BFI] = \frac{975}{79} \cdot 9 \cdot \frac{1}{2} = \frac{8775}{158}.$$

Remark. We will show a faster way to find the smallest of the six segments. In general, for a triangle with side lengths $a \leq b \leq c$, using angle bisector theorem, the lengths of the six segments can be found as $\frac{xy}{y+z}$ where (x, y, z) is a permutation of (a, b, c). Note that the smallest of these is $\frac{ab}{b+c}$ since it gives both the smallest numerator and the largest denominator. When $(a, b, c) = (25, 39, 40)$ we get $\frac{25 \cdot 39}{39+40}$ as before.

23. For positive real number r, the inequality $a^3 + 4b^3 + 3 \geq r(a + b)$ is true for all positive real numbers a and b. What is the largest possible value of r?

(A) $\sqrt{6}$ (B) $\sqrt{8}$ (C) 3   (D) $2\sqrt[3]{4}$ (E) 4

Answer (C): Consider $(a, b) = \left(1, \frac{1}{2}\right)$. This gives $4.5 \geq r \times 1.5$ or $r \leq 3$.

We now show that the inequality is true when $r = 3$. For any three positive numbers x, y, and z, we know by AM-GM inequality that

$$\frac{x^3 + y^3 + z^3}{3} \geq \sqrt[3]{x^3 \cdot y^3 \cdot z^3} = xyz.$$

Using this with $(x, y, z) = (a, 1, 1)$ we get $a^3 + 2 \geq 3a$. Once again using it with $(x, y, z) = (2b, 1, 1)$ we get $8b^3 + 2 \geq 6b$ or $4b^3 + 1 \geq 3b$. Adding the two, we have $a^3 + 4b^3 + 3 \geq 3(a + b)$.

We conclude that $r = 3$ is the largest value for which the given inequality is true for all positive real numbers a and b.

24. Two ants begin at opposite vertices of a cube with side length 1 meter and walk along the edges at 1 meter per second. At each vertex, each ant randomly picks an adjacent edge to transverse (which can be the edge it just came from). What is the expected value of the time, in seconds, it will take them to meet?

(A) 11   (B) 11.5   (C) 12   (D) 12.5   (E) 13

Answer (E): Because of parity, note that after each second, the ants will have a taxicab distance (distance going along the edges) of either 1 or 3. Let E_1 and E_3 be the expected values of the time it will take them to meet when they are 1 unit apart and 3 units apart, respectively. By considering the 9 possible combinations of moves, we can get

$$E_1 = \frac{1}{9} \cdot \frac{1}{2} + \frac{2}{3}(1 + E_1) + \frac{2}{9}(1 + E_3)$$

and

$$E_3 = \frac{2}{3}(1 + E_1) + \frac{1}{3}(1 + E_3).$$

Solving this system of equations, we get $(E_1, E_3) = (11.5, 13)$, so the answer is 13.

25. Define $G_k = 2F_{k+1} - F_k$, where $\{F_k\}$ is the Fibonacci sequence given by $F_0 = 0$, $F_1 = 1$, and $F_k = F_{k-1} + F_{k-2}$ for all $k \geq 2$. If

$$G_1 + G_2 + G_3 + \ldots + G_{2021} = F_a + F_b - F_c$$

for some positive integers $a > b > c$, what is $a + b + c$?

(A) 4049 **(B)** 4050 **(C)** 4051 **(D)** 4052 **(E)** 4053

Answer (B): For $k \geq 1$, we can rewrite G_k as $F_{k+1} + (F_{k+1} - F_k) = F_{k+1} + F_{k-1}$. Then we have

$$\sum_{i=1}^{2021} G_k = \sum_{i=1}^{2021} (F_{k+1} + F_{k-1})$$
$$= \sum_{i=1}^{2021} F_{k+1} + \sum_{i=1}^{2021} F_{k-1}$$

Here, we use the identity $F_1 + F_2 + F_3 + \ldots + F_n = F_{n+2} - 1$, which can be proven by induction. The first sum equals $(F_{2024} - 1) - F_1 = F_{2024} - 2$ and the second sum equals $F_{2022} - 1$. Combining, we obtain

$$\sum_{i=1}^{2021} G_k = (F_{2024} - 2) + (F_{2022} - 1) = F_{2024} + F_{2022} - F_4.$$

Hence $(a, b, c) = (2024, 2022, 4)$ and $a + b + c = 2024 + 2022 + 4 = 4050$.

We will show that it is indeed unique using the following two claims:

Claim 1: If $S = F_a + F_b - F_c$ for some positive integers $a > b > c$, then a is uniquely determined.

Proof. $F_c \leq F_b \leq F_{a-1}$, so we have

$$F_a \leq S < F_a + F_{a-1} = F_{a+1}.$$

Since the intervals $[F_a, F_{a+1})$ for $a = 2, 3, \ldots$ are disjoint and cover all positive integers, knowing S uniquely determines a.

Claim 2: For any positive integer R, as long as neither R nor $R + 1$ is a member of the Fibonacci sequence, R can be written as $F_b - F_c$ with positive integers $b > c$ in at most one way.

Proof. Suppose $R = F_b - F_c$ for some positive integers $b > c$. Note that $c \neq b - 1$ or otherwise $R = F_b - F_{b-1} = F_{b-2}$ would be a term of the Fibonacci sequence. Hence, $c \leq b - 2$ and we have

$$F_{b-1} = F_b - F_{b-2} \leq R = F_b - F_c < F_b.$$

So R lies in $[F_b, F_{b+1})$ for some $b = 2, 3, \ldots$. But these are disjoint intervals and they cover all positive integers, so knowing R uniquely determines b. Now looking at the positive difference $F_b - R$, we find that it cannot be 1, or otherwise $R + 1$ would be a member of the Fibonacci sequence. So $F_b - R \geq 2$ and hence it can only be equal to at most one member of the Fibonacci sequence F_c.

The first claim for the number $S = F_{2024} - F_{2022} - F_4$ shows that any solution $S = F_a + F_b - F_c$ with positive integers $a > b > c$ forces a to be 2024. Then using the second claim with $R = F_{2022} - F_4$ shows that (b, c) can be no other than $(2022, 4)$. Hence, we conclude that $(a, b, c) = (2024, 2022, 4)$ is the only solution.

AMC 10 PRACTICE TESTS VOL 1

TEST-2

INSTRUCTIONS

1. This is a twenty-five question multiple choice test. Each question is followed by answers marked A, B, C, D and E. Only one of these is correct.

2. SCORING. You will receive 6 points for each correct answer, 1.5 points for each problem left unanswered, and 0 points for each incorrect answer.

3. Only scratch paper, graph paper, rulers, protractors, and erasers are allowed as aids. Calculators are NOT allowed. No problems on the test *require* the use of a calculator.

4. Figures are not necessarily drawn to scale.

5. You will have **75 minutes** to complete the test.

1. Kelly gets paid $50 an hour, but she has to pay $50 in taxes for every 8 hours that she works. On average, over an eight-hour period how much does she earn per hour after taxes?

   (A) $40.00   **(B)** $41.25   **(C)** $42.50   **(D)** $43.75   **(E)** $45.00

2. Evan rolls a pair of fair six-sided dice. What is the probability that the sum and product of the two numbers rolled are both even?

   (A) 0   **(B)** $\frac{1}{4}$ **(C)** $\frac{1}{2}$ **(D)** $\frac{3}{4}$ **(E)** 1

3. Stephen can eat a cookie in 10 seconds, and Jiakang can eat a cookie in 15 seconds. How many seconds will it take them to eat 30 cookies together?

   (A) 140   **(B)** 150   **(C)** 165   **(D)** 170   **(E)** 180

4. Let $\{x\}$ denote the sum of the positive divisors of x. For example,

$$\{6\} = 1 + 2 + 3 + 6 = 12.$$

   What is $\{\{\{4\}\}\}$?

   (A) 8   **(B)** 15   **(C)** 16   **(D)** 21   **(E)** 24

5. A rectangle with area 32 is twice as long as it is wide. A circle is drawn inside the rectangle tangent to three sides. What is the area of the circle?

   (A) π **(B)** 2π **(C)** 4π **(D)** 8π **(E)** 16π

6. Which of the following equations has the largest number of real solutions?

   (A) $(x+4)^3 = 0$ **(B)** $\sqrt{-x} - 5 = 0$ **(C)** $|x-2| + 3 = 0$ **(D)** $\sqrt{x-2} + 4 = 0$
   (E) $|x+3| - 4 = 0$

7. After an evening of trick or treating, three sisters, Hanna, Michelle, and Olivia, share their Halloween candies as follows: First, Hanna takes one candy along with one-third of the remaining candies. Then, Michelle takes half of the remaining candies and two more candies after that. Finally, Olivia takes the last three candies. How many candies did they collect?

(A) 13   **(B)** 16   **(C)** 19   **(D)** 22   **(E)** 25

8. Real numbers a and b satisfy $2^{a+2} = 8^{b+8}$ and $3^{a+3} = 9^{b+9}$. What is $a + b$?

(A) -6 **(B)** 2   **(C)** 3   **(D)** 4   **(E)** 6

9. What is the area of the region bounded by $y = ax$, $y = -bx$, and $y = c$ where a, b, and c are positive real numbers?

(A) $\dfrac{ac + bc}{2}$ **(B)** $\dfrac{ac^2 + bc^2}{2}$ **(C)** $\dfrac{c}{2a} + \dfrac{c}{2b}$ **(D)** $\dfrac{a^2c + b^2c}{2}$ **(E)** $\dfrac{c^2}{2a} + \dfrac{c^2}{2b}$

10. What is the largest positive integer n such that 2^n divides $7^8 - 3^8$?

(A) 2   **(B)** 3   **(C)** 4   **(D)** 5   **(E)** 6

11. Andrew, Robert, and Steven are running around a 400-meter circular track. Andrew runs at 3.5 meters per second, Robert runs at 4 meters per second, and Steven runs at 5 meters per second. If they start together and run in the same direction, after how many seconds will they first all meet again?

(A) $266\dfrac{2}{3}$ **(B)** 400   **(C)** 800   **(D)** 1200   **(E)** 1600

12. Given the points $A = (0,0)$ and $B = (2,7)$, let S be the set of points C on the plane such that triangle ABC has area $\sqrt{3}$. Let b be the y-coordinate of an intersection point of S with the line $x = 0$. What is the product of all possible values of b?

(A) -3 **(B)** $-\sqrt{3}$ **(C)** $-\dfrac{3}{4}$ **(D)** $\dfrac{3}{4}$ **(E)** $\sqrt{3}$

13. For a positive integer n, let $\sigma(n)$ denote the sum of the positive factors of n, and $\rho(n)$ denote the sum of the reciprocals of the positive factors of n. How many positive integers n satisfy

$$\sigma(n) = 2022\rho(n)?$$

(A) 0   (B) 1   (C) 2   (D) 4   (E) 8

14. It is the first day of math camp, and Aaron does not know the names of any of the instructors. However, he knows that one of them is Iurie, some of them are named David, and the rest are named Alex. The probability that a randomly chosen instructor is named Alex is $\frac{2}{3}$. The probability that two randomly chosen instructors are both named Alex is $\frac{3}{7}$. What is the probability that three randomly chosen instructors are all named Alex?

(A) $\frac{1}{4}$ (B) $\frac{2}{13}$ (C) $\frac{8}{35}$ (D) $\frac{24}{91}$ (E) $\frac{20}{77}$

15. Jieun is drawing regular polygons with perimeter 6 and finding their areas. Let $A(n)$ denote the area of such a polygon with n sides. What is the smallest value of c such that

$$|A(i) - A(j)| \le c \text{ for all } i, j \ge 3?$$

(A) $\frac{36}{\pi^2} - \sqrt{3}$ (B) $\frac{9}{\pi} - \sqrt{3}$ (C) $\frac{18}{\pi} - 3$ (D) $\frac{36}{\pi} - \frac{3\sqrt{3}}{2}$ (E) $36\pi - 9\sqrt{3}$

16. In a game, Ayla, Bella, and Camila take turns rolling a fair six-sided die. Ayla rolls first, followed by Bella, Camila, Ayla, and so on. The game ends when a player rolls a 1 for the first time, and that player is the winner. What is the probability that Bella wins?

(A) $\frac{1}{3}$ (B) $\frac{1}{4}$ (C) $\frac{25}{76}$ (D) $\frac{30}{91}$ (E) $\frac{36}{109}$

17. Triangle ABC with sides 8, 15 and 17 is given. Let H, I, and O be the orthocenter, incenter and circumcenter of triangle ABC, respectively. What is the area of the triangle OHI?

(A) $\frac{15}{4}$ (B) $\frac{17}{4}$ (C) $\frac{19}{4}$ (D) $\frac{21}{4}$ (E) $\frac{17\sqrt{2}}{4}$

18. What is the sum of all real solutions x to the equation

$$x^3 - 2x^2 + 2x - 1 = \frac{15}{x}?$$

(A) -1 (B) $\frac{\sqrt{15}}{4}$ (C) 1 (D) $1 + \frac{\sqrt{2}}{2}$ (E) 2

19. Three points, A, B, and C, are chosen randomly, uniformly, and independently on a unit circle. What is the probability that the smallest angle of $\triangle ABC$ is at least $30°$?

(A) $\frac{1}{8}$ (B) $\frac{1}{6}$ (C) $\frac{1}{4}$ (D) $\frac{1}{3}$ (E) $\frac{1}{2}$

20. How many real numbers are roots of the quartic polynomial

$$P(y) = 8y^4 - 4y^3 + 6y^2 - y + 1?$$

(A) 0 (B) 1 (C) 2 (D) 3 (E) 4

21. We call a positive integer a *perfect power* if it can be written as m^n for positive integers m and n with $n \geq 2$. How many perfect powers divide 10!?

(A) 16 (B) 25 (C) 30 (D) 32 (E) 36

22. Positive real numbers x, y, and z satisfy $x + y + z = 15$. The minimum possible value of

$$\frac{1}{xy} + \frac{1}{yz}$$

can be written as $\frac{m}{n}$ for relatively prime positive integers m and n. What is $m + n$?

(A) 120 (B) 121 (C) 229 (D) 240 (E) 241

23. Jennifer repeatedly flips a fair coin, and stops when she obtains the same side three times in a row. What is the expected number of coin flips that are different from the previous flip? For example, if she flips the sequence HTHHH, she will have done so twice, with first HT and then TH.

(A) $\dfrac{3}{2}$ (B) 2   (C) $\dfrac{8}{3}$ (D) 3   (E) $\dfrac{9}{2}$

24. A tetrahedron has vertices $(0,0,0)$, $(0,0,1)$, $(0,1,0)$, and $(1,0,0)$. A second tetrahedron has vertices $(0,0,0)$, $(0,0,1)$, $(0,1,1)$, and $(1,0,1)$. What is the volume of the intersection of the two tetrahedra?

(A) $\dfrac{1}{30}$ (B) $\dfrac{1}{24}$ (C) $\dfrac{1}{18}$ (D) $\dfrac{1}{15}$ (E) $\dfrac{1}{12}$

25. Let $A = \{1!,\ 2!,\ 3!,\ldots, 29!,\ 30!\}$. Alice writes the decimal representations of all numbers in set A on a blackboard and erases any trailing zeros at the end of each number. For example, instead of writing the decimal representation of $8! = 40320$, she writes 4032 instead. How many of the 30 numbers on the blackboard have "04" as their rightmost two digits?

(A) 2   (B) 3   (C) 4   (D) 5   (E) 6

Test-2 Answer Key

1. D
2. B
3. E
4. B
5. C
6. E
7. B
8. A
9. E
10. D
11. C
12. A
13. B
14. D
15. B
16. D
17. D
18. C
19. C
20. A
21. E
22. E
23. D
24. B
25. A

Test-2 Solutions

1. Kelly gets paid $50 an hour, but she has to pay $50 in taxes for every 8 hours that she works. On average, over an eight-hour period how much does she earn per hour after taxes?

   (A) $40.00 **(B)** $41.25 **(C)** $42.50 **(D)** $43.75 **(E)** $45.00

   Answer (D): Every eight hours, she earns $400 and pays $50 in taxes. Therefore she keeps $350 for herself. So on average, she earns $\frac{\$350}{8} = \$43.75$ per hour.

2. Evan rolls a pair of fair six-sided dice. What is the probability that the sum and product of the two numbers rolled are both even?

   (A) 0 **(B)** $\frac{1}{4}$ **(C)** $\frac{1}{2}$ **(D)** $\frac{3}{4}$ **(E)** 1

   Answer (B): In order for the sum and product to be even, both numbers must be even. Any rolled number is even half the time, so the probability that both numbers are even is $\frac{1}{2} \times \frac{1}{2} = \frac{1}{4}$.

3. Stephen can eat a cookie in 10 seconds, and Jiakang can eat a cookie in 15 seconds. How many seconds will it take them to eat 30 cookies together?

   (A) 140 **(B)** 150 **(C)** 165 **(D)** 170 **(E)** 180

   Answer (E): In 30 seconds, Stephen can eat 3 cookies, and Jiakang can eat 2 cookies. Thus, together, they eat $2 + 3 = 5$ cookies every 30 seconds. This is equivalent to the rate of 1 cookie every $\frac{30}{5} = 6$ seconds. Thus, the time it takes for them to eat all 30 cookies is $30 \cdot 6 = 180$ seconds.

4. Let $\{x\}$ denote the sum of the positive divisors of x. For example,

$$\{6\} = 1 + 2 + 3 + 6 = 12.$$

What is $\{\{\{4\}\}\}$?

(A) 8   (B) 15   (C) 16   (D) 21   (E) 24

Answer (B): We do the operation repeatedly:

$\{4\} = 1 + 2 + 4 = 7.$
$\{\{4\}\} = \{7\} = 1 + 7 = 8.$
$\{\{\{4\}\}\} = \{8\} = 1 + 2 + 4 + 8 = 15.$

5. A rectangle with area 32 is twice as long as it is wide. A circle is drawn inside the rectangle tangent to three sides. What is the area of the circle?

(A) π (B) 2π (C) 4π (D) 8π (E) 16π

Answer (C): The rectangle is a 4×8 rectangle. The circle thus has diameter 4 and radius 2. The area of the circle is $2^2 \cdot \pi = 4\pi$.

6. Which of the following equations has the largest number of real solutions?

(A) $(x+4)^3 = 0$ (B) $\sqrt{-x} - 5 = 0$ (C) $|x-2| + 3 = 0$ (D) $\sqrt{x-2} + 4 = 0$
(E) $|x+3| - 4 = 0$

Answer (E): $(x+4)^3 = 0$ has -4 as its only solution. $\sqrt{-x} - 5 = 0$ has one solution, namely -25. $|x-2| + 3 = 0$ has no solutions since an absolute value of an expression such as $|x-2|$ can never be negative. $\sqrt{x-2} + 4 = 0$ also has no real solutions because a square root can never be negative. $|x+3| - 4 = 0$ has two solutions, -7 and 1. Therefore, it has the largest number of real solutions.

7. After an evening of trick or treating, three sisters, Hanna, Michelle, and Olivia, share their Halloween candies as follows: First, Hanna takes one candy along with one-third of the remaining candies. Then, Michelle takes half of the remaining candies and two more candies after that. Finally, Olivia takes the last three candies. How many candies did they collect?

(A) 13   **(B)** 16   **(C)** 19   **(D)** 22   **(E)** 25

Answer (B): Since 3 candies are left after Michelle took her share, she took $(2+3)+2 = 7$ candies. This means 10 candies were left after Hanna took her share, so Hanna took $1 + 5 = 6$ candies. We conclude that there were $6 + 10 = 16$ candies at the beginning.

Alternate Solution: If we let C be the initial number of candies,

$$\frac{2}{3}(C - 1) = \frac{2C - 2}{3}$$

candies are left after Hanna's turn, and then

$$\frac{1}{2}\left(\frac{2C - 2}{3}\right) - 2 = \frac{C - 7}{3} = 3$$

candies are left after Michelle's turn. Hence, we find that $C = 16$.

8. Real numbers a and b satisfy $2^{a+2} = 8^{b+8}$ and $3^{a+3} = 9^{b+9}$. What is $a + b$?

(A) -6 **(B)** 2   **(C)** 3   **(D)** 4   **(E)** 6

Answer (A): We have $2^{a+2} = 2^{3(b+8)}$ and $3^{a+3} = 3^{2(b+9)}$. Thus, $a + 2 = 3(b + 8)$ and $a + 3 = 2(b + 9)$. We solve for $(a, b) = (1, -7)$. Thus $a + b = -6$.

9. What is the area of the region bounded by $y = ax$, $y = -bx$, and $y = c$ where a, b, and c are positive real numbers?

(A) $\dfrac{ac + bc}{2}$ **(B)** $\dfrac{ac^2 + bc^2}{2}$ **(C)** $\dfrac{c}{2a} + \dfrac{c}{2b}$ **(D)** $\dfrac{a^2c + b^2c}{2}$ **(E)** $\dfrac{c^2}{2a} + \dfrac{c^2}{2b}$

Answer (E): Both $y = ax$ and $y = -bx$ pass through the origin. Thus, $y = ax$, $y = -bx$, and $y = c$ bound a triangle with a base parallel to the x-axis and a vertex at the origin. We then divide the bounded region into two right triangles along $x = 0$. The left triangle has legs c and $\frac{c}{b}$. The right side has legs c and $\frac{c}{a}$. The total area is then

$$\frac{1}{2}c \cdot \frac{c}{b} + \frac{1}{2}c \cdot \frac{c}{a} = \frac{c^2}{2a} + \frac{c^2}{2b}.$$

10. What is the largest positive integer n such that 2^n divides $7^8 - 3^8$?

(A) 2   (B) 3   (C) 4   (D) 5   (E) 6

Answer (D): Repeatedly factoring as a difference of squares, this becomes

$$(7 - 3)(7 + 3)(7^2 + 3^2)(7^4 + 3^4).$$

The first three terms are 4, 10, and 58. They have 2, 1, and 1 factors of 2, respectively. For the last term we can calculate it as

$$7^4 + 3^4 = 49^2 + 9^2 = 2401 + 81 = 2482 = 2 \times 1241.$$

This has only 1 factor of 2. In total we have $2 + 1 + 1 + 1 = 5$ factors of 2.

Remark. For the last part, alternatively, we can observe that $49^2 = (48 + 1)^2$ and $9^2 = (8 + 1)^2$ are both 1 more than a multiple of 4. So their sum is 2 more than a multiple of 4, which means $7^4 + 3^4$ has only 1 factor of 2.

11. Andrew, Robert, and Steven are running around a 400-meter circular track. Andrew runs at 3.5 meters per second, Robert runs at 4 meters per second, and Steven runs at 5 meters per second. If they start together and run in the same direction, after how many seconds will they first all meet again?

(A) $266\frac{2}{3}$ (B) 400   (C) 800   (D) 1200   (E) 1600

Answer (C): Relative to Andrew, Robert runs 0.5 m/s faster and Steven runs 1.5 m/s faster. This means that Andrew and Robert will meet every $\frac{400}{0.5} = 800$ seconds as this is the time it takes for Robert to lap Andrew. Similarly, Andrew and Steven will meet every $\frac{400}{1.5} = \frac{800}{3}$ seconds. 800 is the smallest multiple of both 800 and $\frac{800}{3}$, so the three runners meet every 800 seconds.

12. Given the points $A = (0,0)$ and $B = (2,7)$, let S be the set of points C on the plane such that triangle ABC has area $\sqrt{3}$. Let b be the y-coordinate of an intersection point of S with the line $x = 0$. What is the product of all possible values of b?

(A) -3 (B) $-\sqrt{3}$ (C) $-\dfrac{3}{4}$ (D) $\dfrac{3}{4}$ (E) $\sqrt{3}$

Answer (A):

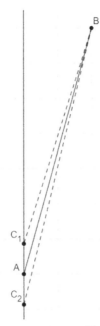

Let $C = (0, b)$ be one of these intersection points. Considering the y-axis as the base of the triangle, the base AC has length $|b|$ and the corresponding height is 2 so the area is $|b|$ which is given to be $\sqrt{3}$. Thus, $b = \pm\sqrt{3}$ and the product of the roots is -3.

Alternate Solution: Using the Shoelace Theorem with triangle ABC, where $C = (0, b)$ as before, we get $\frac{1}{2}|2b - 0| = |b| = \sqrt{3}$. Hence, the answer is $(\sqrt{3}) \cdot (-\sqrt{3}) = -3$.

13. For a positive integer n, let $\sigma(n)$ denote the sum of the positive factors of n, and $\rho(n)$ denote the sum of the reciprocals of the positive factors of n. How many positive integers n satisfy

$$\sigma(n) = 2022\rho(n)?$$

(A) 0 (B) 1 (C) 2 (D) 4 (E) 8

Answer (B): We write each of the terms in $\rho(n)$ with a common denominator: namely

42

the LCM of all factors, or n. For each factor a of n such that $ab = n$, we can write $\frac{1}{a} = \frac{b}{ab} = \frac{b}{n}$. Each possible numerator b is also a factor of n and corresponds to a unique factor a. Thus, summing over all values of $\frac{1}{a}$ and $\frac{b}{n}$, we get that $\rho(n) = \frac{\sigma(n)}{n}$. Thus, $n = 2022$ is the only solution, so the answer is 1.

14. It is the first day of math camp, and Aaron does not know the names of any of the instructors. However, he knows that one of them is Iurie, some of them are named David, and the rest are named Alex. The probability that a randomly chosen instructor is named Alex is $\frac{2}{3}$. The probability that two randomly chosen instructors are both named Alex is $\frac{3}{7}$. What is the probability that three randomly chosen instructors are all named Alex?

(A) $\dfrac{1}{4}$ (B) $\dfrac{2}{13}$ (C) $\dfrac{8}{35}$ (D) $\dfrac{24}{91}$ (E) $\dfrac{20}{77}$

Answer (D): Let a and d denote the number of Alex's and David's respectively. We have:
$$\frac{a}{a+d+1} = \frac{2}{3},$$
$$\frac{a(a-1)}{(a+d+1)(a+d)} = \frac{3}{7}.$$
Dividing the second equation by the first, we find that $\frac{a-1}{a+d} = \frac{9}{14}$. Using this result and the first equation, we get $a = 10$ and $d = 4$. Thus, the desired probability is $\dfrac{\binom{10}{3}}{\binom{15}{3}} = \dfrac{24}{91}$.

Alternate Solution: Let's suppose there are n instructors A of whom are named Alex. The probability that picking an instructor named Alex from those n instructors is $\frac{A}{n} = \frac{2}{3}$. The probability that two randomly chosen instructors are named Alex is then $\frac{A}{n} \cdot \frac{A-1}{n-1} = \frac{3}{7}$. From the first equation, we get $\frac{3}{2}A = n$. Plugging this into the second equation for n and solving yields $A = 10$ and $n = 15$. Thus, the probability that three randomly chosen instructors are all named Alex is simply
$$\frac{10}{15} \cdot \frac{9}{14} \cdot \frac{8}{13} = \frac{24}{91}.$$

15. Jieun is drawing regular polygons with perimeter 6 and finding their areas. Let $A(n)$ denote the area of such a polygon with n sides. What is the smallest value of c such that
$$|A(i) - A(j)| \le c \text{ for all } i, j \ge 3?$$

(A) $\dfrac{36}{\pi^2} - \sqrt{3}$ **(B)** $\dfrac{9}{\pi} - \sqrt{3}$ **(C)** $\dfrac{18}{\pi} - 3$ **(D)** $\dfrac{36}{\pi} - \dfrac{3\sqrt{3}}{2}$ **(E)** $36\pi - 9\sqrt{3}$

Answer (B): We note that the shape with the least area for a fixed perimeter of 6 is an equilateral triangle, and the shapes with the most area approximates a circle with circumference 6.

The shape with the least area for a fixed perimeter of 6 is an equilateral triangle of side length 2, which has area $\dfrac{2^2\sqrt{3}}{4} = \sqrt{3}$.

Jieun can also make shapes whose areas become arbitrarily close to that of a circle with circumference 6. The circle would have radius $\dfrac{6}{2\pi} = \dfrac{3}{\pi}$ and area $\dfrac{9}{\pi}$. We conclude that the smallest value of c is $\dfrac{9}{\pi} - \sqrt{3}$.

16. In a game, Ayla, Bella, and Camila take turns rolling a fair six-sided die. Ayla rolls first, followed by Bella, Camila, Ayla, and so on. The game ends when a player rolls a 1 for the first time, and that player is the winner. What is the probability that Bella wins?

(A) $\dfrac{1}{3}$ **(B)** $\dfrac{1}{4}$ **(C)** $\dfrac{25}{76}$ **(D)** $\dfrac{30}{91}$ **(E)** $\dfrac{36}{109}$

Answer (D): Let a, b, c be probabilities of Ayla, Bella, and Camila winning, respectively. Then, note that $b = \frac{5}{6}a$ since for Bella to win, we need Ayla not to win on the first roll. Similarly, $c = \frac{5}{6}b = \frac{25}{36}a$. Now, since $a + b + c = 1$, we have

$$a\left(1 + \frac{5}{6} + \frac{25}{36}\right) = 1.$$

We find that $a = \frac{36}{91}$, $b = \frac{30}{91}$, and $c = \frac{25}{91}$.

Alternate Solution: We can write an equation just for b by observing that for Bella to win, we need Ayla to roll anything but 1 (with probability $\frac{5}{6}$) and then either Bella wins by rolling 1 (with probability $\frac{1}{6}$) or we need two more non-1 rolls (with probability $\frac{5}{6}$ each) to reset the game to the beginning where Bella has the same chance of winning as before:

$$b = \frac{5}{6}\left(\frac{1}{6} + \frac{5}{6} \cdot \frac{5}{6} \cdot b\right).$$

Solving this linear equation we get $b = \dfrac{30}{91}$.

17. Triangle ABC with sides 8, 15 and 17 is given. Let H, I, and O be the orthocenter, incenter and circumcenter of triangle ABC, respectively. What is the area of the triangle OHI?

(A) $\dfrac{15}{4}$ (B) $\dfrac{17}{4}$ (C) $\dfrac{19}{4}$ (D) $\dfrac{21}{4}$ (E) $\dfrac{17\sqrt{2}}{4}$

Answer (D):

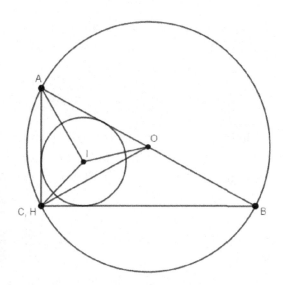

Without loss of generality let $AB = 17$, $BC = 15$ and $AC = 8$. Since $(8, 15, 17)$ is a Pythagorean triple, C is a right angle. This means that $H = C$ and O is the midpoint of AB. Because $BC > AC$ and O is on AB, we see that I is in triangle ACO. The area of $\triangle IHO$ can be calculated as $[IHO] = [ACO] - [ACI] - [AOI]$.

$$[ACO] = \frac{[ABC]}{2} = \frac{8 \times 15}{2 \times 2} = 30.$$

To calculate the area of the other triangles, we need to find the inradius r of triangle ABC which can be calculated from $[ABC] = sr$ where $s = \frac{a+b+c}{2}$. This gives $60 = 20r$ and $r = 3$. Hence,

$$[ACI] = \frac{8 \times 3}{2} = 12$$

and

$$[AOI] = \frac{17}{2} \times 3 \times \frac{1}{2} = \frac{51}{4}.$$

Finally

$$[IHO] = 30 - 12 - \frac{51}{4} = \frac{21}{4}.$$

Alternatively, to find $[CIO]$ let CD be the angle bisector from C. Then

$$\frac{[CIO]}{[CDO]} \times \frac{[CDO]}{[CAB]} = \frac{CI}{CD} \times \frac{DO}{AB}.$$

Using the Angle Bisector Theorem and that O is the midpoint of AB we find that

$$\frac{DO}{AB} = \frac{1}{2} - \frac{AD}{AB} = \frac{1}{2} - \frac{8}{8+15} = \frac{7}{46}.$$

Next using the Angle Bisector Theorem on $\triangle DAC$ we get

$$\frac{CI}{CD} = \frac{AC}{AC+AD} = \frac{8}{8+\frac{8}{23}\cdot 17} = \frac{23}{40}.$$

Combining these, we find

$$[CIO] = 60 \times \frac{23}{40} \times \frac{7}{46} = \frac{21}{4}.$$

Alternate Solution: We can use coordinates. Setting the point $C = H$ as $(0,0)$, we find the inradius as before to give $I = (3,3)$. The circumcenter is simply the midpoint of $A = (0,8)$ and $B = (15,0)$, so $O = (\frac{15}{2}, 4)$. Using the Shoelace Theorem gives $[OHI] = \frac{21}{4}$.

18. What is the sum of all real solutions x to the equation

$$x^3 - 2x^2 + 2x - 1 = \frac{15}{x}?$$

(A) -1 **(B)** $\dfrac{\sqrt{15}}{4}$ **(C)** 1 **(D)** $1 + \dfrac{\sqrt{2}}{2}$ **(E)** 2

Answer (C): Note that the ratio of the coefficients reminds us of the expansion of $(x-1)^5$. We can multiply both sides of the equation by $5x$ to get $5x^4 - 10x^3 + 10x^2 - 5x = 75$. Next, adding $-x^5 + 1$ to both sides of the equation, we have $-(x-1)^5 = -x^5 + 76$, or $x^5 + (1-x)^5 = 76$. The portion of the graph of $x^5 + (1-x)^5$ when $x < \frac{1}{2}$ is monotonically decreasing while the portion when $x > \frac{1}{2}$ is monotonically increasing. Furthermore, 76 is greater than $(\frac{1}{2})^5 - (1 - \frac{1}{2})^5 = \frac{1}{16}$, which is the minimum value of the graph, so there are exactly two real solutions. Notice that if real number r is a solution to this equation, then $1 - r$ is also a solution. Thus, the sum of the solutions is 1.

19. Three points, A, B, and C, are chosen randomly, uniformly, and independently on a unit circle. What is the probability that the smallest angle of $\triangle ABC$ is at least $30°$?

(A) $\dfrac{1}{8}$ (B) $\dfrac{1}{6}$ (C) $\dfrac{1}{4}$ (D) $\dfrac{1}{3}$ (E) $\dfrac{1}{2}$

Answer (C):

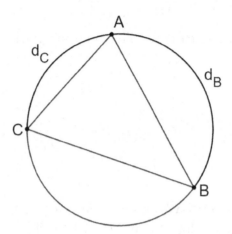

By the Inscribed Angle Theorem, the problem is equivalent to asking for the probability that the smallest arc among AB, BC, and CA is at least $60°$. We use geometric probability. Suppose we fix the first point A. Let B be the closest point to A in the clockwise direction, and let C be the third point. Then, let d_B and d_C be the lengths of minor arcs AB and AC, respectively. Since the points all lie on the same circle, and B does not lie on minor arc AC, $d_B + d_C \le 2\pi$. Therefore, if we plot d_B and d_C on a graph, the set of all possibilities is the region bounded by $d_B = 0$, $d_C = 0$, and $d_B + d_C = 2\pi$.

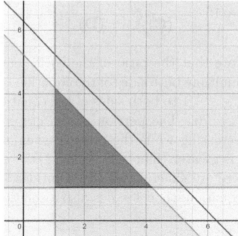

Note that for all angles to be at least $30°$, or $\frac{\pi}{6}$ in radians, then $d_B \ge \frac{\pi}{3}$, $d_C \ge \frac{\pi}{3}$, and

$2\pi - d_B - d_C \geq \frac{\pi}{3}$. In particular, the last equation can be rewritten as $d_B + d_C \geq \frac{5\pi}{3}$. Plotting these conditions, the lines divide our original region to leave a region in the shape of an isosceles right triangle with legs of length π that satisfy the conditions for all angles to be at least $30°$, compared with a total region represented by an isosceles right triangle with legs of length 2π. Thus, the probability of forming a triangle where the smallest angle is at least $30°$ is $\frac{1}{4}$.

20. How many real numbers are roots of the quartic polynomial

$$P(y) = 8y^4 - 4y^3 + 6y^2 - y + 1?$$

(A) 0   (B) 1   (C) 2   (D) 3   (E) 4

Answer (A): To simplify the equation $P(x) = 0$, we double both sides and substitute $x = 2y$. This gives

$$x^4 - x^3 + 3x^2 - x + 2 = 0.$$

Then we proceed to factor this:

$$\begin{aligned} x^4 - x^3 + 3x^2 - x + 2 &= (x^4 + 3x^2 + 2) - (x^3 + x) \\ &= (x^2 + 2)(x^2 + 1) - x(x^2 + 1) \\ &= (x^2 - x + 2)(x^2 + 1) \end{aligned}$$

This has no real solutions, so the answer is 0.

21. We call a positive integer a *perfect power* if it can be written as m^n for positive integers m and n with $n \geq 2$. How many perfect powers divide 10!?

(A) 16   (B) 25   (C) 30   (D) 32   (E) 36

Answer (E): Let m^n be a perfect power divisor of 10!. Since $10! = 2^8 \cdot 3^4 \cdot 5^2 \cdot 7$ we have $2 \leq n \leq 8$ and $m^n = 2^a \cdot 3^b \cdot 5^c \cdot 7^d$ for some integers $0 \leq a \leq 8$, $0 \leq b \leq 4$, $0 \leq c \leq 2$, and $0 \leq d \leq 1$. The numbers a, b, c, d are all multiples of $n \geq 2$ so we first conclude that d cannot be 1 and hence must be 0.

We will next do careful case work based on the values of n. Note that any perfect power can be written as one with a prime power so we just need to consider the n values from $\{2, 3, 5, 7\}$. We have to be extra careful with overcounting problems, especially with the perfect power 1. So in each case, after the first, we will specify how many cases are new:

Case 1: $n = 2$
In this case $a \in \{0, 2, 4, 6, 8\}$, $b \in \{0, 2, 4\}$, and $c \in \{0, 2\}$. There are $5 \times 3 \times 2 = 30$ perfect power divisors in this case.

Case 2: $n = 3$
In this case $a \in \{0, 3, 6\}$, $b \in \{0, 3\}$, and $c = 0$. This leads to $3 \times 2 \times 1 = 6$ cases of which 4 of them are new; $(a, b) = (0, 0)$ and $(6, 0)$ were counted for the $n = 2$ case.

Case 3: $n = 5$
This leads to only one 1 new case $(a, b, c) = (5, 0, 0)$.

Case 4: $n = 7$
This also leads to only one 1 new case $(a, b, c) = (7, 0, 0)$.

Summing these we find that there are $30 + 4 + 1 + 1 = 36$ perfect power divisors of $10!$.

22. Positive real numbers x, y, and z satisfy $x + y + z = 15$. The minimum possible value of
$$\frac{1}{xy} + \frac{1}{yz}$$
can be written as $\frac{m}{n}$ for relatively prime positive integers m and n. What is $m + n$?

(A) 120 **(B)** 121 **(C)** 229 **(D)** 240 **(E)** 241

Answer (E): Note that
$$\frac{1}{xy} + \frac{1}{yz} = \frac{x + z}{xyz} = \frac{15 - y}{y} \cdot \frac{1}{xz}.$$

First fixing y, we note that when $x + z = 15 - y$ is fixed, xz is maximized when x and z are equal (and we wish to maximize xz in order to eventually minimize the desired sum). This gives us
$$\frac{15 - y}{y} \cdot \frac{1}{\left(\frac{15-y}{2}\right)^2} = \frac{4}{y(15 - y)}.$$

Now to maximize $y(15 - y)$, the product of two numbers whose sum is fixed, we need $y = 15 - y = \frac{15}{2}$. Plugging this y we get $\frac{16}{225}$ as the minimal value desired. Hence the answer is $16 + 225 = 241$.

23. Jennifer repeatedly flips a fair coin, and stops when she obtains the same side three times in a row. What is the expected number of coin flips that are different from the previous flip? For example, if she flips the sequence HTHHH, she will have done so twice, with first HT and then TH.

(A) $\dfrac{3}{2}$ (B) 2   (C) $\dfrac{8}{3}$ (D) 3   (E) $\dfrac{9}{2}$

Answer (D): Define $E(k)$ to be the expected number of additional flips different from the last if she starts already having flipped the same outcome k times in a row.

If Jennifer's last flip differed from her second-to-last flip, she has a $\frac{1}{2}$ chance of flipping differently again and increasing her total number of differing flips by 1. She also has a $\frac{1}{2}$ chance of flipping the same outcome again. Thus,

$$E(1) = \frac{1}{2}(E(1) + 1) + \frac{1}{2}E(2).$$

Similarly,

$$E(2) = \frac{1}{2}(E(1) + 1) + \frac{1}{2}E(3) = \frac{1}{2}(E(1) + 1)$$

as Jennifer has a $\frac{1}{2}$ chance of flipping differently from before and a $\frac{1}{2}$ chance of terminating the game by flipping the same outcome a third time.

Solving this system of equations, we compute $E(2) = 2$ and $E(1) = 3$. Note that after 1 flip, Jennifer will always have 0 flips different from "the last one" and will have flipped the same outcome exactly 1 time. Thus, the answer is just $E(1) = 3$.

24. A tetrahedron has vertices $(0,0,0)$, $(0,0,1)$, $(0,1,0)$, and $(1,0,0)$. A second tetrahedron has vertices $(0,0,0)$, $(0,0,1)$, $(0,1,1)$, and $(1,0,1)$. What is the volume of the intersection of the two tetrahedra?

(A) $\dfrac{1}{30}$ (B) $\dfrac{1}{24}$ (C) $\dfrac{1}{18}$ (D) $\dfrac{1}{15}$ (E) $\dfrac{1}{12}$

Answer (B):

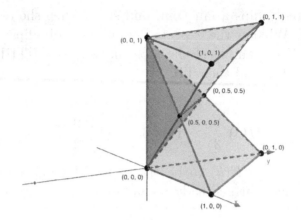

To start with, the two tetrahedra share the vertices $(0,0,0)$ and $(0,0,1)$. To understand the intersection better we will find more intersection points:

The line through $(0,0,1)$ and $(1,0,0)$ intersects the line through $(0,0,0)$ and $(1,0,1)$ at $\left(\frac{1}{2},0,\frac{1}{2}\right)$. Similarly $\left(0,\frac{1}{2},\frac{1}{2}\right)$ is another intersection point.

Thus, the intersection is a tetrahedron with vertices $(0,0,0)$, $(0,0,1)$, $\left(\frac{1}{2},0,\frac{1}{2}\right)$, and $\left(0,\frac{1}{2},\frac{1}{2}\right)$.

Considering the face on plane XZ as the base, this intersection has a height of $\frac{1}{2}$ and a base area of $\frac{1}{2} \cdot 1 \cdot \frac{1}{2} = \frac{1}{4}$, so the volume is

$$\frac{1}{3} \cdot \frac{1}{2} \cdot \frac{1}{4} = \frac{1}{24}.$$

25. Let $A = \{1!,\ 2!,\ 3!, \ldots, 29!,\ 30!\}$. Alice writes the decimal representations of all numbers in set A on a blackboard and erases any trailing zeros at the end of each number. For example, instead of writing the decimal representation of $8! = 40320$, she writes 4032 instead. How many of the 30 numbers on the blackboard have "04" as their rightmost two digits?

(A) 2   (B) 3   (C) 4   (D) 5   (E) 6

Answer (A): It is easy to check the first 10 numbers by hand, finding that only $7! = 5040$ satisfies the condition.

Let $d(n)$ be the units digit of the number obtained from $n!$ when the zeros at the end are erased. If $n+1$ is not a multiple of 5, then we have $d(n+1) \equiv d(n) \times (n+1) \pmod{10}$.

Otherwise, $n + 1 = 5, 10, 15, 20, 25, 30$. Calculating $d(n+1)$ for those numbers one by one:

$$d(15) \equiv \frac{d(13) \times 14 \times 15}{10} = d(13) \times 21 \quad (\mathrm{mod}\ 10).$$

Similarly we find

$$d(20) \equiv d(19) \times 2 \quad (\mathrm{mod}\ 10)$$

$$d(25) \equiv d(23) \times 6 \quad (\mathrm{mod}\ 10)$$

$$d(30) \equiv d(29) \times 3 \quad (\mathrm{mod}\ 10).$$

When we calculate all the values of $d(n)$ for $11 \leq n \leq 30$, we see that only $n = 20, 21, 25, 26, 28$ have $d(n) = 4$. If $t(n)$ is the number of zeros at the end of $n!$, then we must check if these values satisfy $a(n) := \frac{n!}{10^{t(n)}} \equiv 04 \pmod{100}$. This is true when $a(n) \equiv 0 \pmod 4$ and $a(n) \equiv 4 \pmod{25}$. It is easy to see that the first congruence is satisfied for all the possible values of n.

Note that $t(20) = t(21) = 4$, $t(25) = t(26) = 6$, and that for any positive integer m:

$$(5m+1)(5m+2)(5m+3)(5m+4) \equiv -1 \quad (\mathrm{mod}\ 25).$$

Using these we find that

$$a(20) \equiv \frac{(-1)\cdot 1(-1)\cdot 2(-1)\cdot 3\cdot(-1)\cdot 4}{16} \equiv \frac{-1}{16} \equiv 14 \quad (\mathrm{mod}\ 25).$$

$$a(21) \equiv a(20) \times 21 \equiv 14 \times (-4) \equiv 19 \quad (\mathrm{mod}\ 25).$$

Similarly, we get $a(25) \equiv 9 \pmod{25}$, $a(26) \equiv 9 \pmod{25}$, and $a(28) \equiv 4 \pmod{25}$.

We conclude that there are only 2 solutions, namely 7 and 28.

AMC 10 PRACTICE TESTS VOL 1

TEST-3

INSTRUCTIONS

1. This is a twenty-five question multiple choice test. Each question is followed by answers marked A, B, C, D and E. Only one of these is correct.

2. SCORING: You will receive 6 points for each correct answer, 1.5 points for each problem left unanswered, and 0 points for each incorrect answer.

3. Only scratch paper, graph paper, rulers, protractors, and erasers are allowed as aids. Calculators are NOT allowed. No problems on the test *require* the use of a calculator.

4. Figures are not necessarily drawn to scale.

5. You will have **75 minutes** to complete the test.

1. Jamin saves \$150 of his earnings every week to buy a used car that costs \$4000. After how many weeks will Jamin have saved enough money to buy the car?

   (A) 24   **(B)** 25   **(C)** 26   **(D)** 27   **(E)** 28

2. A marathon runner starts a race at 9:30 AM. By 10:10 AM, she has run a quarter of the race. Assuming she runs at a constant speed, at what time will she finish the race?

   (A) 11:30 AM   **(B)** 12:10 PM   **(C)** 12:30 PM   **(D)** 1:20 PM
   (E) 1:50 PM

3. A high school consists of grades 10 through 12 only. The 10th, 11th, and 12th graders can finish an assignment in an average of 10, 8.5, and 7 minutes, respectively. If there are twice as many 11th graders as 12th graders and three times as many 10th graders as 11th graders, what is the average time it takes a student at this school to finish the assignment?

   (A) $8\frac{1}{2}$ **(B)** $8\frac{2}{3}$ **(C)** 9   **(D)** $9\frac{1}{3}$ **(E)** $9\frac{1}{2}$

4. It takes Cara 7 minutes to walk from her house to the grocery store, and 10 minutes to walk from the grocery store to the library. Assuming she always takes the shortest path (a line segment) to her destinations and walks at a constant speed, what is the shortest time, in minutes, it could take her to walk from the library back to her house?

   (A) 0   **(B)** 3   **(C)** 7   **(D)** 10   **(E)** 17

5. Aniketh has a digital stopwatch counting up from 000 to 999, inclusive. On the stopwatch, each digit uses a 7-segment LED display. However, none of the top segments of the digit displays turn off, so the digits 1 and 4 are not displayed properly. A 1 is displayed as a 7 and a 4 is displayed as a 9. At a random time during the 1000-second interval, Aniketh accidentally drops his stopwatch in a pool and it stops. What is the probability that the stopwatch was not displaying a 7 or 9 when it stopped?

   (A) $\dfrac{1}{125}$ **(B)** $\dfrac{8}{125}$ **(C)** $\dfrac{27}{125}$ **(D)** $\dfrac{3}{5}$ **(E)** $\dfrac{64}{125}$

6. In rectangle $ABCD$, sides AB, BC, CD, DA are divided by points E, F, G, and H, respectively, such that

$$AE = 4EB, \ BF = 4FC, \ CG = 4GD, \text{ and } DH = 4HA.$$

Given that $AB = 5$ and $BC = 8$, what is the ratio of the area of $ABCD$ to the area of $EFGH$?

(A) $\dfrac{5}{4}$ (B) $\dfrac{25}{17}$ (C) $\dfrac{3}{2}$ (D) $\dfrac{25}{16}$ (E) $\dfrac{13}{8}$

7. A sequence is defined by $a_1 = 1$ and $a_n = a_{n-1} + \frac{a_{n-1}}{n}$ for $n \geq 2$. What is a_{2023}?

(A) 1010   (B) 1011   (C) 1012   (D) 2023   (E) 2024

8. How many ordered pairs of positive integers (x, y) satisfy the equation

$$x^2 + 4y = 3x + 16?$$

(A) 1   (B) 2   (C) 3   (D) 4   (E) 5

9. What is the remainder when

$$2 + 2^2 + 2^{2^2} + 2^{2^{2^2}} + \ldots + 2^{2^{2^{2^{2^{2^{2^{2^{2^2}}}}}}}}$$

is divided by 5? The sum has 10 terms.

(A) 0   (B) 1   (C) 2   (D) 3   (E) 4

10. The equation $2x^2 - 8x = c$ has two positive real solutions for x. What is the length of the interval for all possible values of c?

(A) 2   (B) 3   (C) 4   (D) 6   (E) 8

11. How many positive integers less than 200 are multiples of 2 or 3 but not both?

    (A) 99   (B) 100   (C) 131   (D) 132   (E) 133

12. Mehmet has a 13×13 checkerboard. Each square is colored with one of three colors (black, gray, and white) so that any three consecutive squares in a row or column contain all three colors. If one of the corner squares is colored black, how many black squares are there in all?

    (A) 25   (B) 55   (C) 56   (D) 57   (E) 58

13. In a certain game, a player rolls a die until a 6 is rolled. For each roll that is not a 6, the player gets the amount of money, in dollars, of the number that came up on the die. How much should the game master charge to make the game a fair game, that is, a game where the expected value of net gain is 0?

    (A) 15   (B) 30   (C) 45   (D) 75   (E) 90

14. Fifteen identical billiard balls are arranged in an equilateral triangle as shown, such that adjacent balls are touching. A "billiards triangle" of negligible thickness completely encloses the billiard balls, as shown. Let A denote the area of the region enclosed by the billiards triangle, and let B denote the area of a circle with the same radius as that of one billiard ball. What is $\frac{A}{B}$?

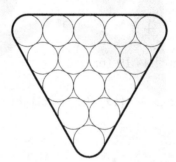

(A) $\dfrac{12 + 4\sqrt{3} + \pi}{\pi}$ (B) $\dfrac{18 + 16\sqrt{3} + \pi}{\pi}$ (C) $\dfrac{18 + 18\sqrt{3} + \pi}{\pi}$

(D) $\dfrac{24 + 16\sqrt{3} + \pi}{\pi}$ (E) $\dfrac{24 + 19\sqrt{3}}{\pi}$

15. A palindrome is an integer whose digits read the same when written in reverse order. What is the largest positive integer in base 10 that divides all 6-digit base 5 palindromes?

   (A) 1   (B) 2   (C) 4   (D) 6   (E) 12

16. A triangle has two sides of lengths 12 and 20. An angle bisector to the third side divides it into two segments of integer lengths. What is the sum of all possible perimeters of the triangle?

   (A) 80   (B) 104   (C) 112   (D) 132   (E) 144

17. A fair 1000-sided die whose faces are labeled with $1, 2, 3, \ldots, 1000$ is rolled twice. If it is known that the two rolls are not the same, what is the probability that the larger one is greater than 750?

   (A) $\dfrac{249}{999}$ (B) $\dfrac{250}{999}$ (C) $\dfrac{583}{1332}$ (D) $\dfrac{125}{222}$ (E) $\dfrac{499}{999}$

18. What is the sum of all integers x such that $1 < ((x-3)^2 - 3)^2 < 200$?

   (A) 21   (B) 22   (C) 24   (D) 30   (E) 33

19. An equilateral triangle is drawn whose vertices are all on the edges of a unit square. What is the difference between the largest and smallest possible areas of the triangle?

   (A) 0   (B) $\dfrac{\sqrt{3}}{16}$ (C) $\dfrac{7\sqrt{3} - 12}{4}$ (D) $\dfrac{2\sqrt{6} - \sqrt{3} - 3}{4}$
   (E) $\dfrac{3\sqrt{2} - \sqrt{6} - \sqrt{3}}{4}$

20. In triangle ABC with sides $AB = 6$ and $AC = 9$, point D is given on side AC such that $AD = 4$. If $\overline{BD}$ and $\overline{BC}$ both have integer lengths, what is the sum of all possible lengths for BC?

    (A) 15   (B) 18   (C) 24   (D) 26   (E) 27

21. On a 2-hour test with 10 problems, the ith problem is worth i points and takes Jimmy $i^2 + 8$ minutes to solve correctly. If Jimmy spends his time wisely, at most how many points can he get?

    (A) 15   (B) 16   (C) 17   (D) 18   (E) 19

22. The number 7^7 is written in binary. What are its first four digits counting from the left?

    (A) 1001   (B) 1010   (C) 1100   (D) 1101   (E) 1110

23. There exist n equally spaced points on the circumference of a unit circle. When two points are randomly chosen, the probability that they will have distance greater than $\sqrt{3}$ is $\frac{11}{31}$. If the probability that the distance between two randomly chosen points is greater than $\sqrt{2}$ is $\frac{p}{q}$ where p and q are relatively prime positive integers, what is $p + q + n$?

    (A) 70   (B) 72   (C) 74   (D) 76   (E) 78

24. Square $ABCD$ has side length 1. Distinct points E_1 and E_2 are in the same plane as the square such that $AE_1 = AE_2 = 6$ and $CE_1 = CE_2 = 5$. What is $BE_1^2 + BE_2^2$?

    (A) 60   (B) 61   (C) 62   (D) 63   (E) 64

25. Let a_n be a sequence of integers satisfying $a_2 = 3a_1$ and $a_n = 4a_{n-1} + 7a_{n-2}$ for all positive integers $n \geq 3$. If $a_{14} = 1764761883$ and $a_{15} = 9382576859$, then what are the last two digits of

$$a_1 + a_2 + \ldots + a_{14}?$$

(A) 04   (B) 24   (C) 44   (D) 64   (E) 84

Test-3 Answer Key

1. D
2. B
3. D
4. B
5. C
6. B
7. C
8. B
9. E
10. E
11. A
12. D
13. A
14. D
15. D
16. B
17. C
18. A
19. C
20. E
21. D
22. C
23. E
24. B
25. A

Test-3 Solutions

1. Jamin saves \$150 of his earnings every week to buy a used car that costs \$4000. After how many weeks will Jamin have saved enough money to buy the car?

   (A) 24   **(B)** 25   **(C)** 26   **(D)** 27   **(E)** 28

   Answer (D): $\frac{4000}{150} = \frac{80}{3}$ is between 26 and 27, so it will take 27 weeks to accumulate at least \$4000.

2. A marathon runner starts a race at 9:30 AM. By 10:10 AM, she has run a quarter of the race. Assuming she runs at a constant speed, at what time will she finish the race?

   (A) 11:30 AM   **(B)** 12:10 PM   **(C)** 12:30 PM   **(D)** 1:20 PM
   (E) 1:50 PM

   Answer (B): She ran a quarter of the race in 40 minutes. At this rate, she will run the remaining three-quarters in $3 \times 40 = 120$ minutes, or 2 hours. Hence, she will finish the race 2 hours after 10:10 AM, which is 12:10 PM.

3. A high school consists of grades 10 through 12 only. The 10th, 11th, and 12th graders can finish an assignment in an average of 10, 8.5, and 7 minutes, respectively. If there are twice as many 11th graders as 12th graders and three times as many 10th graders as 11th graders, what is the average time it takes a student at this school to finish the assignment?

   (A) $8\frac{1}{2}$ **(B)** $8\frac{2}{3}$ **(C)** 9   **(D)** $9\frac{1}{3}$ **(E)** $9\frac{1}{2}$

   Answer (D): The ratio of students in grades 10, 11, and 12 is $6 : 2 : 1$, respectively.

63

The average time is then the weighted average

$$\frac{6 \times 10 + 2 \times 8.5 + 1 \times 7}{6 + 2 + 1} = \frac{84}{9} = 9\frac{1}{3}.$$

4. It takes Cara 7 minutes to walk from her house to the grocery store, and 10 minutes to walk from the grocery store to the library. Assuming she always takes the shortest path (a line segment) to her destinations and walks at a constant speed, what is the shortest time, in minutes, it could take her to walk from the library back to her house?

(A) 0   (B) 3   (C) 7   (D) 10   (E) 17

Answer (B): Let t be the time it takes Cara to travel from the library back to her house. By the triangle inequality (including degenerate triangles), $10 \leq 7 + t$, so $t \geq 3$. The shortest time $t = 3$ is achieved when Cara's house is on the line segment joining the grocery store and the library and lies between them (degenerate triangle case).

5. Aniketh has a digital stopwatch counting up from 000 to 999, inclusive. On the stopwatch, each digit uses a 7-segment LED display. However, none of the top segments of the digit displays turn off, so the digits 1 and 4 are not displayed properly. A 1 is displayed as a 7 and a 4 is displayed as a 9. At a random time during the 1000-second interval, Aniketh accidentally drops his stopwatch in a pool and it stops. What is the probability that the stopwatch was not displaying a 7 or 9 when it stopped?

(A) $\dfrac{1}{125}$ (B) $\dfrac{8}{125}$ (C) $\dfrac{27}{125}$ (D) $\dfrac{3}{5}$ (E) $\dfrac{64}{125}$

Answer (C): Each digit has a $1 - \frac{4}{10} = \frac{3}{5}$ chance of showing up as neither a 7 nor a 9. The cumulative probability that no digit displays a 7 or a 9 is

$$\left(\frac{3}{5}\right)^3 = \frac{27}{125}.$$

6. In rectangle $ABCD$, sides AB, BC, CD, DA are divided by points E, F, G, and H, respectively, such that

$$AE = 4EB, \ BF = 4FC, \ CG = 4GD, \ \text{and} \ DH = 4HA.$$

Given that $AB = 5$ and $BC = 8$, what is the ratio of the area of $ABCD$ to the area of $EFGH$?

(A) $\dfrac{5}{4}$ (B) $\dfrac{25}{17}$ (C) $\dfrac{3}{2}$ (D) $\dfrac{25}{16}$ (E) $\dfrac{13}{8}$

Answer (B):

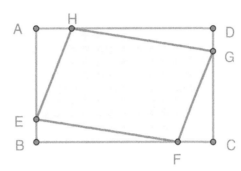

The area of $EFGH$ can be found by subtracting the areas of the four right triangles AEH, BEF, CFG, and DGH from the area of $ABCD$. Each of these triangles has area

$$\frac{1}{2} \times \frac{1}{5} \times \frac{4}{5} \times [ABCD] = \frac{2}{25} \times [ABCD].$$

Thus, the area of $EFGH$ is equal to

$$\left(1 - 4 \times \frac{2}{25}\right) \times [ABCD] = \frac{17}{25} \times [ABCD].$$

Our desired ratio is

$$\frac{[ABCD]}{[EFGH]} = \frac{25}{17}.$$

7. A sequence is defined by $a_1 = 1$ and $a_n = a_{n-1} + \frac{a_{n-1}}{n}$ for $n \geq 2$. What is a_{2023}?

(A) 1010   (B) 1011   (C) 1012   (D) 2023   (E) 2024

Answer (C): Observe that

$$a_n = a_{n-1} + \frac{a_{n-1}}{n} = \frac{n+1}{n} \times a_{n-1}.$$

Thus,

$$\frac{a_n}{n+1} = \frac{a_{n-1}}{n} = \cdots = \frac{a_1}{2} = \frac{1}{2} \implies a_n = \frac{n+1}{2}.$$

In particular, $a_{2023} = 1012$.

Alternate Solution: Plugging in small numbers for n in the recurrence relation we observe that the terms $a_1 = 1$, $a_2 = \frac{3}{2}$, $a_3 = 2, \ldots$ follow the pattern of the arithmetic sequence: $a_n = \frac{n+1}{2}$. We can then check to ensure that this pattern will continue. If $a_n = \frac{n+1}{2}$, then:

$$a_{n+1} = a_n + \frac{a_n}{n+1} = \frac{n+1}{2} + \frac{1}{2} = \frac{(n+1)+1}{2}.$$

Hence, a_n is indeed $\frac{n+1}{2}$ for all positive integers n and $a_{2023} = 1012$.

8. How many ordered pairs of positive integers (x, y) satisfy the equation

$$x^2 + 4y = 3x + 16?$$

(A) 1   (B) 2   (C) 3   (D) 4   (E) 5

Answer (B): We rewrite the equation as $x(x - 3) = 16 - 4y$. Since $y \geq 1$, we have $16 - 4y \leq 12$, which leads to $x(x - 3) \leq 12$. This is true only when $x \leq 5$. By trying the first five positive integers, we can see that only $x = 3$ and $x = 4$ yield integer y values ($y = 4$ and $y = 3$, respectively). Hence, there are 2 solutions.

9. What is the remainder when

$$2 + 2^2 + 2^{2^2} + 2^{2^{2^2}} + \ldots + 2^{2^{2^{2^{2^{2^{2^{2^{2^2}}}}}}}}$$

is divided by 5? The sum has 10 terms.

(A) 0   (B) 1   (C) 2   (D) 3   (E) 4

Answer (E): We inspect the remainder of each term when divided by 5. Starting with the third term, they are all 16 raised to a power, so they all have remainder 1 when divided by 5. Hence, the remainder of the original sum is the same as the remainder of $2 + 4 + 8 \times 1 = 14$ which gives an answer of 4.

10. The equation $2x^2 - 8x = c$ has two positive real solutions for x. What is the length of the interval for all possible values of c?

(A) 2   **(B)** 3   **(C)** 4   **(D)** 6   **(E)** 8

Answer (E): Completing the square, we have $2(x-2)^2 = c + 8$. Letting $k = c + 8$, we have $2(x-2)^2 = k$. Thus, $k \geq 0$. The roots are symmetric around 2. Since both of the roots are positive they must be in the $(0, 4)$ interval. This means $|x - 2| < 2$ and $k = 2(x-2)^2 < 8$. Moreover any number k in the interval $(0, 8)$ leads to two positive roots: $x = 2 \pm \sqrt{\frac{k}{2}}$. Finally, the interval for c is just a shift of the interval of k so it has the same length and the answer is 8.

Alternate Solution: We first complete the square, similar to above. We can then visualize the graph of $y = 2(x-2)^2$ and observe that only the horizontal lines $y = k$ for $k \in (0, 8)$ intersect the graph at two points, giving the same answer.

11. How many positive integers less than 200 are multiples of 2 or 3 but not both?

(A) 99   **(B)** 100   **(C)** 131   **(D)** 132   **(E)** 133

Answer (A): There are 99 multiples of 2, 66 multiples of 3, and 33 multiples of 6 (multiples of both 2 and 3) less than 200. So there are $99 - 33 = 66$ multiples of 2 but not 3 and $66 - 33 = 33$ multiples of 3 but not 2. Adding these, we find $66 + 33 = 99$ multiples of 2 or 3 but not both.

12. Mehmet has a 13×13 checkerboard. Each square is colored with one of three colors (black, gray, and white) so that any three consecutive squares in a row or column contain all three colors. If one of the corner squares is colored black, how many black squares are there in all?

(A) 25   **(B)** 55   **(C)** 56   **(D)** 57   **(E)** 58

Answer (D): Note that, excluding one of the black corners, the remaining squares can be grouped into black-gray-white triples. Hence, exactly one third of these grouped squares are black. So there are $\frac{13^2 - 1}{3} + 1 = 57$ black squares.

13. In a certain game, a player rolls a die until a 6 is rolled. For each roll that is not a 6, the player gets the amount of money, in dollars, of the number that came up on the

die. How much should the game master charge to make the game a fair game, that is, a game where the expected value of net gain is 0?

(A) 15   (B) 30   (C) 45   (D) 75   (E) 90

Answer (A): Let D be the number of dollars charged for a fair game. Then the player paying D dollars is expected to gain the same amount back from the game. We first find out what the expected earnings are from just the first roll.

If the player rolls a 6 with probability $\frac{1}{6}$ the game ends with no earnings. With the remaining $\frac{5}{6}$ chance, the player earns 1, 2, 3, 4, or 5 dollars, each equally likely, so on average the player earns 3 dollars. Hence, the expected earnings from the first roll are $\frac{5}{6} \times 3 = 2.5$ dollars. So D is 2.5 plus what the player is expected to earn from the second round onward. However, this is simply $\frac{5}{6} \times D$ since to earn anything after the first round, the first roll has to be a non-6 number with probability $\frac{5}{6}$ and after that point the game is the same as the original game, hence gives the same expected earnings. So we get the following equation:

$$D = 2.5 + \frac{5}{6} \times D.$$

Solving this gives $D = 15$.

Alternate Solution: The problem could be solved by noticing that the player expects to roll a 6 after rolling the dice 6 times. In the process, the player rolls from (1, 2, 3, 4, 5) an expected 5 times. Thus, the expected amount of money that the person wins is

$$5 \cdot \left(\frac{1 + 2 + 3 + 4 + 5}{5} \right) = 15.$$

14. Fifteen identical billiard balls are arranged in an equilateral triangle as shown, such that adjacent balls are touching. A "billiards triangle" of negligible thickness completely encloses the billiard balls, as shown. Let A denote the area of the region enclosed by the billiards triangle, and let B denote the area of a circle with the same radius as that of one billiard ball. What is $\frac{A}{B}$?

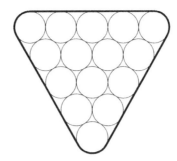

(A) $\dfrac{12 + 4\sqrt{3} + \pi}{\pi}$ (B) $\dfrac{18 + 16\sqrt{3} + \pi}{\pi}$ (C) $\dfrac{18 + 18\sqrt{3} + \pi}{\pi}$

(D) $\dfrac{24 + 16\sqrt{3} + \pi}{\pi}$ (E) $\dfrac{24 + 19\sqrt{3}}{\pi}$

Answer (D): Observe that since we are comparing a ratio of two areas, the radius does not matter, so we can assume without loss of generality that each billiard ball has radius 1, and we will compute A and B assuming radius 1. In this case, we obtain $B = \pi \cdot 1^2 = \pi$. To find A, we can split up the area enclosed by the billiards triangle into an equilateral triangle, three congruent rectangles, and three $120°$ sectors as shown:

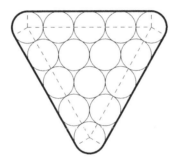

The equilateral triangle has side length 8, so its area is $\frac{8^2\sqrt{3}}{4} = 16\sqrt{3}$. The area of the three rectangles is $3 \times 8 \times 1 = 24$, and the combined area of the three sectors is $\pi \cdot 1^2 = \pi$. Then $A = 24 + 16\sqrt{3} + \pi$ and

$$\frac{A}{B} = \frac{24 + 16\sqrt{3} + \pi}{\pi},$$

or approximately 17.5.

15. A palindrome is an integer whose digits read the same when written in reverse order. What is the largest positive integer in base 10 that divides all 6-digit base 5 palindromes?

(A) 1   (B) 2   (C) 4   (D) 6   (E) 12

Answer (D): The 6-digit palindrome $abccba_5$ when expanded in base 10 is equal to

$$5^5a + 5^4b + 5^3b + 5^2c + 5b + a = a(5^5 + 1) + b(5^4 + 5) + c(5^3 + 5^2)$$
$$= 6(521a + 105b + 25c).$$

Thus, the desired number must be a multiple of 6. However, note that the greatest common divisor is not larger than 6, as the two palindromes 344443_5 and 400004_5 differ by only 6_{10} or 11_5. So our answer is 6.

16. A triangle has two sides of lengths 12 and 20. An angle bisector to the third side divides it into two segments of integer lengths. What is the sum of all possible perimeters of the triangle?

(A) 80   (B) 104   (C) 112   (D) 132   (E) 144

Answer (B): Note that by the Angle Bisector Theorem, the ratio of the lengths of the two segments is $\frac{12}{20} = \frac{3}{5}$. So the two segments have lengths $3s$ and $5s$ for some positive integer s. By the triangle inequality $20 - 12 < (3s + 5s) < 20 + 12$ or $1 < s < 4$. Thus, the possible integer values of s are 2 and 3. The perimeters of these triangles are $32 + 8s$ which can be 48 or 56, summing to 104.

17. A fair 1000-sided die whose faces are labeled with $1, 2, 3, \ldots, 1000$ is rolled twice. If it is known that the two rolls are not the same, what is the probability that the larger one is greater than 750?

(A) $\dfrac{249}{999}$ (B) $\dfrac{250}{999}$ (C) $\dfrac{583}{1332}$ (D) $\dfrac{125}{222}$ (E) $\dfrac{499}{999}$

Answer (C): There are $\binom{1000}{2}$ possible outcomes each being equally likely. We use complementary counting. There are $\binom{750}{2}$ ways for both to be at most 750.

Thus, the probability of the larger being at most 750 is

$$\frac{\binom{750}{2}}{\binom{1000}{2}} = \frac{749}{1332}.$$

The probability that the larger is greater than 750 is

$$1 - \frac{749}{1332} = \frac{583}{1332}.$$

18. What is the sum of all integers x such that $1 < ((x-3)^2 - 3)^2 < 200$?

    (A) 21   **(B)** 22   **(C)** 24   **(D)** 30   **(E)** 33

    Answer (A): We have

    $$2 \le |(x-3)^2 - 3| \le 14.$$

    Then,

    $$(x-3)^2 \in [-11, 1] \cup [5, 17].$$

    Hence, $x - 3 \in \{-4, -3, -1, 0, 1, 3, 4\}$ and $x \in \{-1, 0, 2, 3, 4, 6, 7\}$. The sum of x values is 21.

    The last part of the solution can be done a little faster. Since there are 7 values for $x - 3$ and they are symmetric around 0, the sum of $x - 3$ values is 0. Hence, the sum of x values is $3 \cdot 7 = 21$.

19. An equilateral triangle is drawn whose vertices are all on the edges of a unit square. What is the difference between the largest and smallest possible areas of the triangle?

    (A) 0   **(B)** $\dfrac{\sqrt{3}}{16}$ **(C)** $\dfrac{7\sqrt{3} - 12}{4}$ **(D)** $\dfrac{2\sqrt{6} - \sqrt{3} - 3}{4}$

    (E) $\dfrac{3\sqrt{2} - \sqrt{6} - \sqrt{3}}{4}$

    Answer (C):

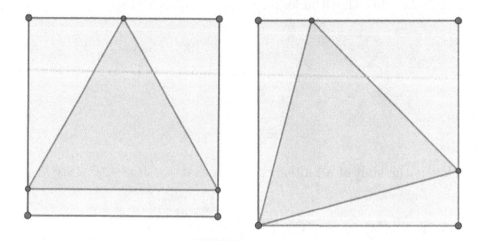

Since two vertices of the triangle must be on opposite edges of the square, the smallest possible side length of the triangle is 1. This is achievable as shown in the left figure above when the first point is the midpoint of the top side and the other two points are on the adjacent sides that are both 1 away from the first point.

The largest side length can be obtained as shown in the right figure above by taking the first point of the triangle to be at a corner of the unit square and the other two points on the two sides not touching the first point.

Indeed, any other equilateral triangle can be transformed into this triangle by a sequence of translations, rotations, and enlargements (dilations) as follows:

Start with an equilateral triangle and first move one of its vertices to a corner of the square by a translation. Next, if neither of the other two vertices are touching a side, enlarge the triangle via a dilation about the first vertex until one of them touches a side. Finally, if the third vertex is not touching a side, rotate and enlarge the triangle until it does.

Now to calculate the side length d of the largest equilateral triangle, observe that d is the hypotenuse of a $15 - 75 - 90$ triangle with the larger leg being 1. The ratios of a $15 - 75 - 90$ triangle can be found as $1 : 2 + \sqrt{3} : \sqrt{6} + \sqrt{2}$ by drawing a segment from the 75 degree angle, splitting it into $15 + 60$ degrees, and dividing the triangle into $30 - 60 - 90$ and $15 - 15 - 150$ triangles. Hence, the hypotenuse we are looking for is $d = \frac{\sqrt{6}+\sqrt{2}}{2+\sqrt{3}} = \sqrt{6} - \sqrt{2}$.

Alternatively, one can also find d by noting that the $15 - 75 - 90$ triangle formed at the lower right corner of the square has base 1, height $1 - \frac{d}{\sqrt{2}}$, and hypotenuse d. Then, the Pythagorean Theorem can be used to find h.

Finally, the difference between the two areas is

$$\frac{(\sqrt{6}-\sqrt{2})^2\sqrt{3}}{4} - \frac{1^2\sqrt{3}}{4} = \frac{8\sqrt{3}-12}{4} - \frac{\sqrt{3}}{4} = \frac{7\sqrt{3}-12}{4}.$$

20. In triangle ABC with sides $AB = 6$ and $AC = 9$, point D is given on side AC such that $AD = 4$. If $\overline{BD}$ and $\overline{BC}$ both have integer lengths, what is the sum of all possible lengths for BC?

    (A) 15   **(B)** 18   **(C)** 24   **(D)** 26   **(E)** 27

    Answer (E): Note that the triangles ABC and ADB are similar since they share $\angle A$ and

    $$\frac{AB}{AD} = \frac{AC}{AB} = \frac{3}{2}.$$

    Therefore, we can let $BD = 2n$ and $BC = 3n$. Since both $2n$ and $3n$ are integers, n must also be an integer and $BC = 3n$ is a multiple of 3. From the triangle inequality on ABC, we get $3 < BC < 15$. Hence, the sum of possible values for BC is $6+9+12 = 27$.

    Alternate Solution: Let $BC = x$ and $BD = y$. Then, we can apply Stewart's Theorem to triangle ABC:

    $$5 \times 4 \times 9 + 9y^2 = 6^2 \times 5 + 4x^2$$
    $$180 + 9y^2 = 180 + 4x^2$$
    $$9y^2 = 4x^2$$
    $$3y = 2x.$$

    Now, because BD and BC are both integers, y must be a multiple of 2, and x must be a multiple of 3. Again, the triangle inequality on $\triangle ABC$ gives $3 < x < 15$. Thus, the sum of all possible values of $x = BC$ is $6 + 9 + 12 = 27$.

21. On a 2-hour test with 10 problems, the ith problem is worth i points and takes Jimmy $i^2 + 8$ minutes to solve correctly. If Jimmy spends his time wisely, at most how many points can he get?

    (A) 15   **(B)** 16   **(C)** 17   **(D)** 18   **(E)** 19

Answer (D): By solving problems 3, 4, 5, and 6, Jimmy scores 18 points. We show this is maximal.

Problems 1 and 2 have a total of 3 points, so if the 6th problem is the highest problem solved, problems 3 through 6 will need to be solved in order to score at least 18 points. However, these 4 problems take 118 minutes to solve, so there is not enough time to solve another problem.

Let the "efficiency" of a problem be the number of points earned divided by the time in minutes it takes to solve the problem. Then, the efficiency of problem i is $\frac{i}{i^2+8}$, which obtains a maximum of $\frac{1}{4\sqrt{2}}$ at $i = 2\sqrt{2}$. Therefore, as $i > 3$ increases, the efficiency decreases.

The most efficient problem from problem 7 to problem 10 is also the one that takes the least time. This is problem 7, which takes 57 minutes to solve. This leaves 63 minutes to solve problems at a rate less than $\frac{1}{4\sqrt{2}}$ points per minute, during which less than $\frac{63}{4\sqrt{2}} < 12$ points can be scored. This means if a problem between 7 and 10 is solved, less than 19 points can be scored. Therefore, 18 points is the maximum possible points Jimmy can get.

22. The number 7^7 is written in binary. What are its first four digits counting from the left?

(A) 1001   (B) 1010   (C) 1100   (D) 1101   (E) 1110

Answer (C): By the Binomial Theorem,

$$7^7 = (8-1)^7 = 8^7 - 7 \cdot 8^6 + 21 \cdot 8^5 - 35 \cdot 8^4 + 35 \cdot 8^3 - 21 \cdot 8^2 + 7 \cdot 8 - 1.$$

Simplified, this is

$$25 \cdot 8^5 + 11 \cdot 8^3 - 21 \cdot 8^2 + 56 - 1.$$

Further simplified, we have

$$(2^4 + 2^3 + 2^0) \cdot 2^{15} + (2^3 + 2^1 + 2^0) \cdot 2^9 - (2^4 + 2^2 + 2^0) \cdot 2^6 + (2^5 + 2^4 + 2^2 + 2^1 + 2^0).$$

The digits of the term $(2^3 + 2^1 + 2^0) \cdot 2^9$ are too small to affect the first four digits of $25 \cdot 8^5$ in base 2, so the first four digits are precisely those of 25 in base 2: they are 1100.

23. There exist n equally spaced points on the circumference of a unit circle. When two points are randomly chosen, the probability that they will have distance greater than $\sqrt{3}$ is $\frac{11}{31}$. If the probability that the distance between two randomly chosen points is greater than $\sqrt{2}$ is $\frac{p}{q}$ where p and q are relatively prime positive integers, what is $p + q + n$?

(A) 70   (B) 72   (C) 74   (D) 76   (E) 78

Answer (E): We consider the probability that the two points will have distance less than or equal to $\sqrt{3}$. This is equivalent to the probability that the two points will be less than or equal to 120 degrees apart.

We compute the probability as follows: After picking the first point, we have $n - 1$ choices for the next point, and $2\lfloor \frac{n}{3} \rfloor$ of them are within the necessary angle, since two-thirds of the circle is within 120 degrees of the first point (rounding down if 120 degrees from the first point lands between two other points).

Therefore the probability that the distance is less than or equal to $\sqrt{3}$ is $\frac{2\lfloor \frac{n}{3} \rfloor}{n-1}$, so the probability of it being greater than $\sqrt{3}$ is $1 - \frac{2\lfloor \frac{n}{3} \rfloor}{n-1}$. Setting this equal to $\frac{11}{31}$ and writing $n = 3q + r$ where r is the remainder when n is divided by 3, the equation simplifies to $q = 10(r - 1)$. The only positive solution comes from $r = 2$ giving $q = 10$ and $n = 32$.

Performing similar work as above tells us that the probability of the distance being greater than $\sqrt{2}$ is $1 - \frac{2\lfloor \frac{n}{4} \rfloor}{n-1} = \frac{15}{31}$.

Thus, $p = 15$, $q = 31$, and $n = 32$, giving $p + q + n = 78$.

24. Square $ABCD$ has side length 1. Distinct points E_1 and E_2 are in the same plane as the square such that $AE_1 = AE_2 = 6$ and $CE_1 = CE_2 = 5$. What is $BE_1^2 + BE_2^2$?

(A) 60   (B) 61   (C) 62   (D) 63   (E) 64

Answer (B): Assume without loss of generality that E_1 is closer to B than E_2 is, as in the following diagram:

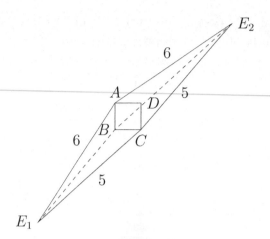

We observe that the figure is symmetric about AC, so $BE_2 = DE_1$, and it suffices to compute $BE_1^2 + DE_1^2$.

We use the property that given a square $ABCD$ and any point E in the same plane as the square, we have $AE^2 + CE^2 = BE^2 + DE^2$; this can be verified by the Pythagorean theorem.

Applying this property, we obtain $BE_1^2 + DE_1^2 = AE_1^2 + CE_1^2 = 6^2 + 5^2 = 61$.

25. Let a_n be a sequence of integers satisfying $a_2 = 3a_1$ and $a_n = 4a_{n-1} + 7a_{n-2}$ for all positive integers $n \geq 3$. If $a_{14} = 1764761883$ and $a_{15} = 9382576859$, then what are the last two digits of

$$a_1 + a_2 + \ldots + a_{14}?$$

(A) 04   (B) 24   (C) 44   (D) 64   (E) 84

Answer (A): Let
$$S = a_1 + a_2 + \ldots a_{14}.$$

We set up the equations:

$$a_{15} = 4a_{14} + 7a_{13},$$
$$a_{14} = 4a_{13} + 7a_{12},$$
$$\vdots$$
$$a_3 = 4a_2 + 7a_1.$$

By adding these equations together, we get

$$S + a_{15} - a_2 - a_1 = 4S - 4a_1 + 7S - 7a_{14}.$$

Solving this for S and using $a_2 = 3a_1$ we get

$$S = \frac{3a_1 - a_2 + 7a_{14} + a_{15}}{10} = \frac{7a_{14} + a_{15}}{10}.$$

We are given a_{14} and a_{15}, so we substitute them into our expression for S to find

$$S = \frac{7 \cdot 883 + 859}{10} \equiv 04 \pmod{100}.$$

Note: letting $a_1 = 1$ and $a_2 = 3$ produces a valid sequence with the given conditions.

AMC 10 PRACTICE TESTS VOL 1

TEST-4

INSTRUCTIONS

1. This is a twenty-five question multiple choice test. Each question is followed by answers marked A, B, C, D and E. Only one of these is correct.

2. SCORING: You will receive 6 points for each correct answer, 1.5 points for each problem left unanswered, and 0 points for each incorrect answer.

3. Only scratch paper, graph paper, rulers, protractors, and erasers are allowed as aids. Calculators are NOT allowed. No problems on the test *require* the use of a calculator.

4. Figures are not necessarily drawn to scale.

5. You will have **75 minutes** to complete the test.

1. Sara is having a party and is buying lunch for all the guests. She must pay a base fee of $45 for catering plus $4.50 per sandwich and $0.50 per drink. If Sara wants to buy a sandwich and a drink for each of the 200 guests, how much will she pay?

   (A) $245　　(B) $1000　　(C) $1045　　(D) $1050　　(E) $2045

2. Let A and B be defined as follows:

$$A = 2 - 4 + 6 - 8 + \cdots + 2022 - 2024$$
$$B = 3 - 5 + 7 - 9 + \cdots + 2023 - 2025.$$

   What is $B - A$?

   (A) -1012　　(B) -1　　(C) 0　　(D) 1　　(E) 1012

3. Suppose 5 candy canes are worth the same as 2 chocolates, and 4 caramels are worth the same as 3 candy canes. How many chocolates are 30 caramels worth?

   (A) 9　　(B) 15　　(C) 18　　(D) 30　　(E) 36

4. A square with side length 12 is cut along both diagonals, forming four pieces. The four pieces are then rearranged to form two congruent squares. What is the side length of one of these squares?

   (A) 3　　(B) $3\sqrt{2}$　　(C) 6　　(D) $6\sqrt{2}$　　(E) 9

5. Kelsey wants to buy a computer. The computer costs $400, and her allowance is $10 a week. She decides to save half of her weekly allowance for the computer. If she starts saving when she gets her allowance today, and she gets a weekly allowance every 7 days, how many days from now will she be able to buy the computer?

   (A) 273　　(B) 280　　(C) 546　　(D) 553　　(E) 560

6. How many positive integers less than 1000 with distinct digits are divisible by 5?

    (A) 146   (B) 153   (C) 154   (D) 163   (E) 164

7. The perimeter of a rectangle is 24 and its area is 16. What is the positive difference between the width and the length of the rectangle?

    (A) $6\sqrt{2}$ (B) $5\sqrt{3}$ (C) $4\sqrt{5}$ (D) $3\sqrt{10}$ (E) $16\sqrt{2}$

8. Brian has some coins in his pockets. 75% of the coins are quarters and the rest are nickels. If the number of quarters triples and the number of nickels doubles, which of the following would be closest to the percentage of the total value of the coins that comes from the nickels?

    (A) 4%   (B) 5%   (C) 6%   (D) 7%   (E) 8%

9. A quadrilateral $ABCD$ has three congruent angles. If $\angle A = 75°$, what is the sum of all possible values for $\angle B$?

    (A) 135°   (B) 170°   (C) 210°   (D) 230°   (E) 305°

10. How many ordered pairs of positive integers (x, y) satisfy

$$2(xy + 60) = (x + 8)(y + 8)?$$

    (A) 4   (B) 6   (C) 8   (D) 10   (E) 12

82

11. Aaron has an ordered list A of 10 numbers whose first element is 2. Brianna creates an ordered list B of 9 numbers by subtracting the ith number from the $(i+1)^{\text{th}}$ number in A, for $i = 1, 2, 3, \ldots, 9$. Carl creates an ordered list C of 8 numbers by subtracting the ith number from the $(i+1)^{\text{th}}$ number in B, for $i = 1, 2, 3, \ldots, 8$. Carl's list is $(1, -2, 3, -4, 5, -6, 7, -8)$. If the last element in B is 5, what is the last element in A?

(A) 75   (B) 77   (C) 79   (D) 81   (E) 83

12. What is the shape of the graph of $(x+y)^3 = x^3 + y^3$ in the Cartesian plane?

(A) three points
(B) a line
(C) two parallel lines
(D) three intersecting lines
(E) a circle

13. A leap year occurs when the year number is a multiple of 4 but not 100, or when it is a multiple of 400. The Declaration of Independence was unanimously approved on July 2, 1776. Given that July 2, 2020 was a Thursday, what day of the week was the Declaration approved on?

(A) Monday   (B) Tuesday   (C) Wednesday   (D) Thursday   (E) Friday

14. Points A and B lie on a circle with center O such that $\angle AOB = 120°$. A second circle is internally tangent to the first circle and tangent to the segments $\overline{OA}$ and $\overline{OB}$. What is the ratio of the radius of the first circle to the radius of the second circle?

(A) 2   (B) $\dfrac{3+2\sqrt{3}}{3}$ (C) $\dfrac{5\sqrt{3}}{3}$ (D) 3   (E) $\dfrac{7\sqrt{3}-3}{3}$

15. How many positive integers have the same number of digits when written in base 3 as in base 4?

(A) 7   (B) 17   (C) 18   (D) 22   (E) 35

16. What is the maximum number of (possibly overlapping) triangles formed by 8 lines, given that 3 of the lines are parallel?

    (A) 40   **(B)** 44   **(C)** 48   **(D)** 52   **(E)** 55

17. In a doubles tournament, each team consists of two players. 144 players are participating in a quadruple-elimination doubles tennis tournament, where each match has only one winning team and each team is eliminated after the fourth loss. The matches are continued until there is only one team left. What is the greatest number of matches played in the tournament?

    (A) 284   **(B)** 285   **(C)** 286   **(D)** 287   **(E)** 288

18. Real numbers a, b, c satisfy the system of equations

    $$a + 3b + 6c = 20$$
    $$3a + 6b + 10c = 8$$
    $$6a + 10b + 15c = 12$$

    What is $15a + 21b + 29c$?

    (A) -76 **(B)** 68   **(C)** 152   **(D)** 160   **(E)** 244

19. Four real numbers are given whose pairwise sums are $22, 25, 27, 29, 31$, and 34. Let N denote the sum of all possible products of these four numbers. What is the remainder when N is divided by 1000?

    (A) 200   **(B)** 696   **(C)** 720   **(D)** 896   **(E)** 920

20. Lazar repeatedly flips a fair coin. What is the expected number of heads he will flip before flipping two consecutive tails?

    (A) 2   **(B)** $\dfrac{5}{2}$ **(C)** 3   **(D)** 4   **(E)** $\dfrac{9}{2}$

21. Andrew has written the integers 1 through 6 on a board in some order. He writes the average of each set of two consecutive numbers on the board in a row below the two original numbers to create a new set of five numbers. He then repeats this process with the resulting numbers until he is left with a row containing a single number. What is the positive difference between the largest and smallest possible values for the last number?

(A) $\frac{5}{4}$ (B) $\frac{3}{2}$ (C) $\frac{7}{4}$ (D) 2   (E) $\frac{9}{4}$

22. Let n be the smallest integer greater than 1 such that the decimal representation of 17^n ends in 17. What is n?

(A) 11   (B) 21   (C) 41   (D) 51   (E) 101

23. What is the value of the infinite sum

$$\frac{(1-1)3^1}{(1+2)!} + \frac{(2-1)3^2}{(2+2)!} + \frac{(3-1)3^3}{(3+2)!} + \ldots + \frac{(n-1)3^n}{(n+2)!} + \ldots?$$

(A) $\frac{1}{2}$ (B) $\frac{3}{4}$ (C) 1   (D) $\frac{3}{2}$ (E) 3

24. A cone of height 12 and radius 5 is placed in the middle of three mutually tangent spheres that are all congruent to each other so that each sphere is externally tangent to the cone and all four objects are resting on the same surface, with the cone's base flat on the surface. A cylinder, also with its base flat on the surface, is internally tangent to all three spheres (so the cylinder contains the spheres). What is the radius of the cylinder?

(A) $\frac{15 + 5\sqrt{3}}{2}$ (B) $10\sqrt{3}$ (C) $\frac{45 + 25\sqrt{3}}{4}$ (D) $15 + 5\sqrt{3}$ (E) 24

25. How many positive integers less than 200 are divisible by the number of its positive divisors?

(A) 19   (B) 20   (C) 22   (D) 24   (E) 25

Test-4 Answer Key

1. C
2. C
3. A
4. D
5. D
6. C
7. C
8. A
9. E
10. B
11. E
12. D
13. B
14. B
15. E
16. A
17. D
18. D
19. D
20. C
21. E
22. B
23. D
24. C
25. E

Test-4 Solutions

1. Sara is having a party and is buying lunch for all the guests. She must pay a base fee of $45 for catering plus $4.50 per sandwich and $0.50 per drink. If Sara wants to buy a sandwich and a drink for each of the 200 guests, how much will she pay?

   (A) $245   **(B)** $1000   **(C)** $1045   **(D)** $1050   **(E)** $2045

   Answer (C): She will pay $45 + 200 \times ($4.50 + $0.50) = 1045.

2. Let A and B be defined as follows:

   $$A = 2 - 4 + 6 - 8 + \cdots + 2022 - 2024$$
   $$B = 3 - 5 + 7 - 9 + \cdots + 2023 - 2025.$$

   What is $B - A$?

   (A) -1012 **(B)** -1 **(C)** 0 **(D)** 1 **(E)** 1012

   Answer (C): Subtracting the corresponding terms in A from B, we get

   $$
   \begin{aligned}
   B - A &= (3 - 2) + (-5 - (-4)) + \cdots + (2023 - 2022) + (-2025 - (-2024)) \\
   &= 1 + (-1) + \cdots + 1 + (-1) = 0.
   \end{aligned}
   $$

3. Suppose 5 candy canes are worth the same as 2 chocolates, and 4 caramels are worth the same as 3 candy canes. How many chocolates are 30 caramels worth?

   (A) 9   **(B)** 15   **(C)** 18   **(D)** 30   **(E)** 36

   Answer (A): Each caramel is worth $\frac{3}{4}$ of a candy cane, and each candy cane is worth $\frac{2}{5}$ of a chocolate. Therefore, each caramel is worth $\frac{3}{4} \times \frac{2}{5} = \frac{3}{10}$ of a chocolate. Thus, 30 caramels are worth $\frac{3}{10} \times 30 = 9$ chocolates.

4. A square with side length 12 is cut along both diagonals, forming four pieces. The four pieces are then rearranged to form two congruent squares. What is the side length of one of these squares?

(A) 3   (B) $3\sqrt{2}$ (C) 6   (D) $6\sqrt{2}$ (E) 9

Answer (D): Note that each new square has side length one-half the length of the diagonal of the original square, or

$$\frac{1}{2} \times \left(12\sqrt{2}\right) = 6\sqrt{2}.$$

5. Kelsey wants to buy a computer. The computer costs \$400, and her allowance is \$10 a week. She decides to save half of her weekly allowance for the computer. If she starts saving when she gets her allowance today, and she gets a weekly allowance every 7 days, how many days from now will she be able to buy the computer?

(A) 273   (B) 280   (C) 546   (D) 553   (E) 560

Answer (D): Every week, she saves \$5 dollars, so to save \$400 dollars, she will need to save for 80 weeks. Since she started saving today, she will need to wait 79 more weeks or $7 \times 79 = 553$ days.

6. How many positive integers less than 1000 with distinct digits are divisible by 5?

(A) 146   (B) 153   (C) 154   (D) 163   (E) 164

Answer (C): We will do casework based on the number of digits. Note that the last digit must be either 0 or 5.

Case 1: The integer has one digit. In this case, the only possible value is 5.

Case 2: The integer has two digits. If the units digit is 0, then there are 9 choices for the first digit. If the units digit is 5, then there are 8 choices for the first digit. In total, there are $9 + 8 = 17$ numbers satisfying the condition for this case.

Case 3: The integer has three digits. If the units digit is 0, then there are 9 choices for the first digit and 8 choices for the second digit. If the units digit is 5, then there are 8 choices for the first digit and 8 choices for the second digit. In total, there are $9 \times 8 + 8 \times 8 = 136$ numbers for this case.

Altogether, there is a total of $1 + 17 + 136 = 154$ positive integers that satisfy the given conditions.

7. The perimeter of a rectangle is 24 and its area is 16. What is the positive difference between the width and the length of the rectangle?

(A) $6\sqrt{2}$ **(B)** $5\sqrt{3}$ **(C)** $4\sqrt{5}$ **(D)** $3\sqrt{10}$ **(E)** $16\sqrt{2}$

Answer (C): Let the length and width be a and b. We have $a + b = 12$ and $ab = 16$. Then,
$$(a - b)^2 = (a + b)^2 - 4ab = 144 - 4 \cdot 16 = 80.$$
Hence, $|a - b| = 4\sqrt{5}$.

8. Brian has some coins in his pockets. 75% of the coins are quarters and the rest are nickels. If the number of quarters triples and the number of nickels doubles, which of the following would be closest to the percentage of the total value of the coins that comes from the nickels?

(A) 4%   **(B)** 5%   **(C)** 6%   **(D)** 7%   **(E)** 8%

Answer (A): Initially, the ratio of quarters to nickels is $3 : 1$. If the number of quarters triples and the number of nickels doubles, the ratio becomes $9 : 2$. Thus, the percentage of the total value of the coins that comes from the nickels is
$$\frac{2 \times 5}{9 \times 25 + 2 \times 5} = \frac{2}{47} \approx 4\%.$$

9. A quadrilateral $ABCD$ has three congruent angles. If $\angle A = 75°$, what is the sum of all possible values for $\angle B$?

(A) $135°$ (B) $170°$ (C) $210°$ (D) $230°$ (E) $305°$

Answer (E): Three of the angles are congruent. There are 3 possibilities for the fourth angle: It is either $\angle A$, $\angle B$ or one of the remaining angles. In these cases, we get $\angle B$ is $95°$, $135°$ and $75°$, respectively. Hence, the sum of possible values for $\angle B$ is $305°$.

10. How many ordered pairs of positive integers (x, y) satisfy

$$2(xy + 60) = (x + 8)(y + 8)?$$

(A) 4   (B) 6   (C) 8   (D) 10   (E) 12

Answer (B): Expanding both sides, we have

$$2xy + 120 = xy + 8x + 8y + 64.$$

Rearranging and simplifying gives

$$xy - 8x - 8y + 56 = 0.$$

Using Simon's Favorite Factoring Trick, we can rewrite this equation as:

$$(x - 8)(y - 8) = 8.$$

Because x and y are positive integers, $(x - 8)$ and $(y - 8)$ must both be divisors of 8 greater than -8. Checking such factorings of 8, we find the following 6 pairs for $(x - 8, y - 8)$:

$$(1, 8), \ (2, 4), \ (4, 2), \ (8, 1), \ (-2, -4), \ (-4, -2).$$

Note that the factorings $(-2) \cdot (-4)$ and $(-4) \cdot (-2)$ are easy to miss but they also give positive integers x, y. Hence, the answer is 6.

11. Aaron has an ordered list A of 10 numbers whose first element is 2. Brianna creates an ordered list B of 9 numbers by subtracting the ith number from the $(i + 1)^{\text{th}}$ number in A, for $i = 1, 2, 3, \ldots, 9$. Carl creates an ordered list C of 8 numbers by subtracting

the ith number from the $(i+1)^{\text{th}}$ number in B, for $i = 1, 2, 3, \ldots, 8$. Carl's list is $(1, -2, 3, -4, 5, -6, 7, -8)$. If the last element in B is 5, what is the last element in A?

(A) 75 **(B)** 77 **(C)** 79 **(D)** 81 **(E)** 83

Answer (E): By iterating backwards from 5, we can solve for B. Note that the ith number in B is equal to $(5 - \sum_{n=i}^{8} n\text{th element of } C)$, for $i = 1, 2, 3, \ldots, 8$. Thus,

$$B = (9, 10, 8, 11, 7, 12, 6, 13, 5).$$

Similarly, by iterating forward from 2, we can find that

$$A = (2, 11, 21, 29, 40, 47, 59, 65, 78, 83).$$

So the answer is 83.

12. What is the shape of the graph of $(x+y)^3 = x^3 + y^3$ in the Cartesian plane?

 (A) three points
 (B) a line
 (C) two parallel lines
 (D) three intersecting lines
 (E) a circle

Answer (D): Expanding, we get

$$x^3 + 3x^2y + 3xy^2 + y^3 = x^3 + y^3.$$

So $3x^2y + 3xy^2 = 0$, which factors as $3xy(x+y) = 0$. Thus, either $x = 0$, $y = 0$, or $y = -x$, so the graph consists of three lines that intersect at the origin.

13. A leap year occurs when the year number is a multiple of 4 but not 100, or when it is a multiple of 400. The Declaration of Independence was unanimously approved on July 2, 1776. Given that July 2, 2020 was a Thursday, what day of the week was the Declaration approved on?

(A) Monday   (B) Tuesday   (C) Wednesday   (D) Thursday   (E) Friday

Answer (B): Every year has 52 weeks and one more day, except leap years have an extra day. There are 244 years from 1776 to 2020. Among these, there are 61 that are multiples of 4 (not counting 1776 since the given date is after February 29th). Two of these 61 are multiples of 100 (1800 and 1900), so they are not leap years. Hence, there are 59 leap years between 1776 and 2020. This gives us $244 + 59 = 303$ days, or 43 weeks and two additional days. Because July 2nd, 2020 was a Thursday, July 2nd, 1776 occurred two days before Thursday, which is a Tuesday.

14. Points A and B lie on a circle with center O such that $\angle AOB = 120°$. A second circle is internally tangent to the first circle and tangent to the segments $\overline{OA}$ and $\overline{OB}$. What is the ratio of the radius of the first circle to the radius of the second circle?

(A) 2   (B) $\dfrac{3 + 2\sqrt{3}}{3}$ (C) $\dfrac{5\sqrt{3}}{3}$ (D) 3   (E) $\dfrac{7\sqrt{3} - 3}{3}$

Answer (B):

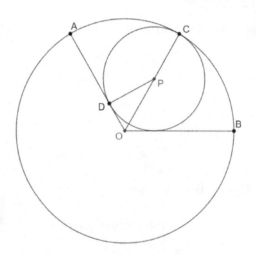

Suppose the two circles are tangent at C, and the center of the second circle is P. Also, suppose the second circle intersects $\overline{OA}$ at D. By symmetry, C is halfway between A and B on arc AB, so $\angle AOC = 60°$. Then OPD is a 30-60-90 triangle. Let R and r be the radii of the larger and smaller circles, respectively. Then $OP = R - r$ and $PD = r$. Thus, $R - r = \frac{2\sqrt{3}}{3}r$, so $\frac{R}{r} = \frac{3 + 2\sqrt{3}}{3}$.

15. How many positive integers have the same number of digits when written in base 3 as in base 4?

(A) 7 **(B)** 17 **(C)** 18 **(D)** 22 **(E)** 35

Answer (E): An integer in base 3 will always have at least as many digits as the same number in base 4. Consider the numbers with n digits in both base 3 and base 4. The largest n-digit number in base 3 is $3^n - 1$, while the smallest n-digit number in base 4 is 4^{n-1}. Thus, there are $(3^n - 1) - (4^{n-1}) + 1 = 3^n - 4^{n-1}$ numbers with n digits in both bases (this is an inclusive range). Note that this assumes that $4^{n-1} < 3^n - 1$. If this value is negative, then there are no numbers with n digits in both base 3 and base 4. Computing $3^n - 4^{n-1}$ for the first few values of n gives 2, 5, 11, 17, -13,... After $n = 4$, there are no numbers that have n digits in both bases. Thus, the answer is the sum for $n \in \{1, 2, 3, 4\}$, which is $2 + 5 + 11 + 17 = 35$.

16. What is the maximum number of (possibly overlapping) triangles formed by 8 lines, given that 3 of the lines are parallel?

(A) 40 **(B)** 44 **(C)** 48 **(D)** 52 **(E)** 55

Answer (A): There are five lines without any restrictions, so in order to maximize the number of triangles, these lines must all intersect each other. Thus, any set of three of these lines will form a triangle. From these lines, we can obtain $\binom{5}{3} = 10$ triangles. No triangle can contain two parallel sides, so the rest of the triangles are formed by one of the three parallel lines and two of the other five lines for $\binom{3}{1} \times \binom{5}{2} = 3 \times 10 = 30$ triangles. There are a total of $10 + 30 = 40$ triangles.

Alternate Solution: We will use complementary counting. There are a total of $\binom{8}{3} = 56$ sets of three lines. Of these, there is one set of three parallel lines, as well as $\binom{3}{2} \times 5 = 15$ sets containing two parallel lines and one of the five other lines. Thus, in total there are 16 sets cannot form a triangle. Subtracting this from the total number of sets of three lines, we obtain a total of $56 - 16 = 40$ triangles.

17. In a doubles tournament, each team consists of two players. 144 players are participating in a quadruple-elimination doubles tennis tournament, where each match has only one winning team and each team is eliminated after the fourth loss. The matches are continued until there is only one team left. What is the greatest number of matches played in the tournament?

(A) 284   **(B)** 285   **(C)** 286   **(D)** 287   **(E)** 288

Answer (D): There are 72 teams. As each game results in a win and a loss, and each loss dictates which team is eliminated, let us consider the total number of losses. We need $71 \times 4 = 284$ matches for 71 teams to each lose 4 times, after which they are eliminated. The last team standing could have lost at most 3 matches. Therefore, at most $284 + 3 = 287$ matches were played in the tournament.

18. Real numbers a, b, c satisfy the system of equations

$$a + 3b + 6c = 20$$
$$3a + 6b + 10c = 8$$
$$6a + 10b + 15c = 12$$

What is $15a + 21b + 29c$?

(A) -76 **(B)** 68   **(C)** 152   **(D)** 160   **(E)** 244

Answer (D): Subtract twice the second equation from the sum of the first and third equations to get $a + b + c = 16$.

Now, adding twice the second equation to 9 times $a + b + c$ gives us the desired sum, which is

$$2 \times 8 + 9 \times 16 = 160.$$

19. Four real numbers are given whose pairwise sums are $22, 25, 27, 29, 31,$ and 34. Let N denote the sum of all possible products of these four numbers. What is the remainder when N is divided by 1000?

(A) 200   **(B)** 696   **(C)** 720   **(D)** 896   **(E)** 920

Answer (D): Let $a \leq b \leq c \leq d$ be the given numbers. The smallest pairwise sums are $a + b = 22$ and $a + c = 25$. The largest pairwise sums are $b + d = 31$ and $c + d = 34$. From these we get that $c - b = 3$. The remaining ones are $\{a + d, b + c\} = \{27, 29\}$ in some order. That is, $b + c$ is either 27 or 29. Solving for b and c in both cases, we get either $(b, c) = (12, 15)$ or $(13, 16)$. Now, solving for a, d we get (a, b, c, d) is either $(10, 12, 15, 19)$ or $(9, 13, 16, 18)$. The sum of possible products is

$$N = (10 \times 12 \times 15 \times 19) + (9 \times 13 \times 16 \times 18) = 34200 + 33696 = 67896,$$

so the final answer is 896.

20. Lazar repeatedly flips a fair coin. What is the expected number of heads he will flip before flipping two consecutive tails?

(A) 2   (B) $\dfrac{5}{2}$ (C) 3   (D) 4   (E) $\dfrac{9}{2}$

Answer (C): Let E_0 be the expected number of heads that Lazar flips given that either the current flip is the first flip or the previous flip was a head, and let E_1 be the expected number of heads that Lazar flips given that the previous flip was a tail. Looking at the two possibilities for the current flip, we can set up the following equations:

$$E_0 = \frac{1 + E_0}{2} + \frac{0 + E_1}{2}$$

and

$$E_1 = \frac{1 + E_0}{2} + \frac{0}{2}.$$

By solving the two equations, we get that $E_1 = 2$ and $E_0 = 3$. Thus, the expected number of heads he will flip before flipping two consecutive tails is 3.

Alternate Solution: Let E be the answer. The cases for the first one or two flips are: H, TH, and TT, with probabilities $\frac{1}{2}$, $\frac{1}{4}$, and $\frac{1}{4}$, respectively. Considering what happens to E in each of these cases, we get the following equation:

$$E = \frac{1}{2}(E + 1) + \frac{1}{4}(E + 1) + \frac{1}{4} \cdot 0.$$

Solving this, we find that $E = 3$.

21. Andrew has written the integers 1 through 6 on a board in some order. He writes the average of each set of two consecutive numbers on the board in a row below the two original numbers to create a new set of five numbers. He then repeats this process with the resulting numbers until he is left with a row containing a single number. What is the positive difference between the largest and smallest possible values for the last number?

(A) $\dfrac{5}{4}$ (B) $\dfrac{3}{2}$ (C) $\dfrac{7}{4}$ (D) 2   (E) $\dfrac{9}{4}$

Answer (E): When there are two numbers, the final value is the weighted average of the two numbers, where the weights are $1, 1$. When there are three numbers, the weights are $1, 2, 1$. We observe the following:

Claim: In a list of n numbers, the weights are the $(n-1)$th row of Pascal's triangle.

Proof. We use induction on n. This is clearly true for $n = 2$. Suppose the inductive hypothesis is true for integers 1 to $n - 1$. We now show it is true for integers 1 to n.

By the inductive hypothesis, we know that the weights for the first $n-1$ integers are the $(n-2)$th row of Pascal's triangle, and similarly, the weights for the last $n-1$ integers are the $(n-2)$th row of Pascal's triangle. Adding up the corresponding weights gives us

$$\binom{n-2}{0}, \binom{n-2}{1} + \binom{n-2}{0}, \ldots, \binom{n-2}{n-2} + \binom{n-2}{n-1}, \binom{n-2}{n-2},$$

which we can simplify using Pascal's Identity to get

$$\binom{n-1}{0}, \binom{n-1}{2}, \ldots, \binom{n-1}{n-1},$$

completing the induction.

Therefore, with six numbers, the weights are $1, 5, 10, 10, 5, 1$. The largest possible final value occurs when the larger numbers are in the center. Likewise, the smallest possible final value occurs when the smaller numbers are in the center. Thus, the largest possible value for the final number is

$$1 \cdot \frac{1}{2^5} + 3 \cdot \frac{5}{2^5} + 5 \cdot \frac{10}{2^5} + 6 \cdot \frac{10}{2^5} + 4 \cdot \frac{5}{2^5} + 2 \cdot \frac{1}{2^5} = \frac{148}{32} = \frac{37}{8}.$$

The smallest possible value is

$$5 \cdot \frac{1}{2^5} + 3 \cdot \frac{5}{2^5} + 1 \cdot \frac{10}{2^5} + 2 \cdot \frac{10}{2^5} + 4 \cdot \frac{5}{2^5} + 6 \cdot \frac{1}{2^5} = \frac{76}{32} = \frac{19}{8}.$$

The difference is $\frac{37}{8} - \frac{19}{8} = \frac{9}{4}$.

22. Let n be the smallest integer greater than 1 such that the decimal representation of 17^n ends in 17. What is n?

(A) 11   (B) 21   (C) 41   (D) 51   (E) 101

Answer (B): We want $17^n \equiv 17 \pmod{100}$, which means $17^{n-1} \equiv 1 \pmod{100}$. By the Chinese Remainder Theorem, this is equivalent to $17^{n-1} \equiv 1 \pmod{4}$ and $17^{n-1} \equiv 1 \pmod{25}$. The congruence modulo 4 is immediate since $17 \equiv 1 \pmod{4}$.

For $17^{n-1} \equiv 1 \pmod{25}$, we first need $17^{n-1} \equiv 1 \pmod 5$. However, $17^{n-1} \equiv 2^{n-1}$ (mod 5), which is congruent to 1 modulo 5 only when $n-1$ is a multiple of 4.

This means 17^{n-1} must be a power of 17^4, so we look at 17^4 and its powers modulo 25:

$$17^4 \equiv 289^2 \equiv 14^2 = 196 \equiv -4 \pmod{25}.$$

Now looking at powers of -4 mod 25, we find that $(-4)^5 = -1024 \equiv 1 \pmod{25}$, and 5 is the smallest positive integer k such that $(-4)^k \equiv 1 \pmod{25}$. This means that the smallest possible $n-1$ that satisfies $17^{n-1} \equiv 1 \pmod{25}$ is $n-1 = 4 \times 5 = 20$. Hence, by CRT, the smallest desired value of n is 21.

Alternate Solution: Note that the powers of 7 modulo 100 repeat every 4 terms $(7^4 = 2401)$. Now,

$$17^n = (7+10)^n = 7^n + n \cdot 7^{n-1} \cdot 10 + \binom{n}{2} 7^{n-2} \cdot 10^2 + \cdots.$$

Since only the last two terms affect the last two digits of 17^n, we can disregard the rest of the terms. Thus, we are looking for the smallest integer n such that $7^n + n \cdot 7^{n-1} \cdot 10$ ends in 17. Since the units digit must be 7, and the second term doesn't affect the units digit of the sum, $7^n \equiv 1 \pmod{10}$, so $n \equiv 1 \pmod 4$.

Let $n = 4k+1$ for some k. Then, we have

$$7^{4k+1} + (4k+1) \cdot 7^{4k} \cdot 10 \equiv 17 \pmod{100}$$
$$7 + (4k+1) \cdot 10 \equiv 17 \pmod{100}$$
$$(4k+1)10 \equiv 10 \pmod{100}.$$

Thus, $4k+1 \equiv 1 \pmod{10}$, so $k \equiv 0 \pmod 5$. Since $k > 0$, $k = 5$ is the smallest possible value for k, so $4(5)+1 = 21$ is the smallest possible value for n.

23. What is the value of the infinite sum

$$\frac{(1-1)3^1}{(1+2)!} + \frac{(2-1)3^2}{(2+2)!} + \frac{(3-1)3^3}{(3+2)!} + \ldots + \frac{(n-1)3^n}{(n+2)!} + \ldots?$$

(A) $\dfrac{1}{2}$ (B) $\dfrac{3}{4}$ (C) 1 (D) $\dfrac{3}{2}$ (E) 3

Answer (D): We can rewrite the given summation as follows and observe that it telescopes:

$$\sum_{n=1}^{\infty} \frac{(n-1)3^n}{(n+2)!} = \sum_{n=1}^{\infty} \frac{(n+2)3^n - 3 \cdot 3^n}{(n+2)!}$$

$$= \sum_{n=1}^{\infty} \frac{3^n}{(n+1)!} - \sum_{n=1}^{\infty} \frac{3^{n+1}}{(n+2)!}$$

$$= \sum_{n=1}^{\infty} \frac{3^n}{(n+1)!} - \sum_{n=2}^{\infty} \frac{3^n}{(n+1)!}$$

$$= \frac{3^1}{(1+1)!}$$

$$= \frac{3}{2}.$$

24. A cone of height 12 and radius 5 is placed in the middle of three mutually tangent spheres that are all congruent to each other so that each sphere is externally tangent to the cone and all four objects are resting on the same surface, with the cone's base flat on the surface. A cylinder, also with its base flat on the surface, is internally tangent to all three spheres (so the cylinder contains the spheres). What is the radius of the cylinder?

(A) $\dfrac{15 + 5\sqrt{3}}{2}$ (B) $10\sqrt{3}$ (C) $\dfrac{45 + 25\sqrt{3}}{4}$ (D) $15 + 5\sqrt{3}$ (E) 24

Answer (C):

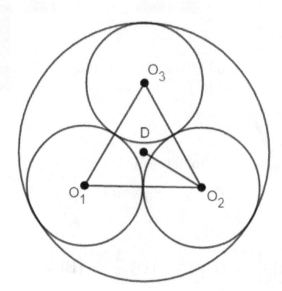

Let the spheres have radius r. By taking a cross-section containing all three sphere centers, we can determine that the centers form an equilateral triangle and are each a distance of $\frac{2r}{\sqrt{3}}$ from the center.

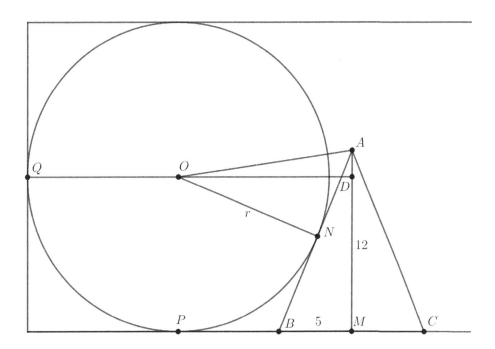

Now, consider a cross-section containing the axis of the cone and the center of one of the spheres. In this cross-section, the sphere, cone, and cylinder become a circle, triangle, and rectangle respectively. Let A be the apex of the triangle, and let O be the center of the circle. Then, let B be the vertex on the base of the triangle which is closer to the circle, let M be the midpoint of the base of the triangle, and let D be the point on AM such that $OD \perp AM$. Let N be the point of tangency between the circle and triangle, and let P be the point of tangency between the circle and the rectangle such that P is on the surface that the solids rest on. Finally, let Q be the point of tangency between the circle and the rectangle such that $\overline{OQ}$ is parallel to the cylinder's bases. Note that the radius of the cylinder is DQ.

We have earlier determined that $OD = \frac{2r}{\sqrt{3}}$. We see that $AD = 12 - r$, so

$$AO = \sqrt{\frac{4r^2}{3} + r^2 - 24r + 144}.$$

Because $\angle ANO$ is a right angle,

$$AN = \sqrt{AO^2 - ON^2} = \sqrt{\frac{4r^2}{3} - 24r + 144} \quad (1)$$

However, $BN = BP = MN - BM = \frac{2r}{\sqrt{3}} - 5$, and $AB = 13$ by the Pythagorean Theorem, so

$$AN = AB - BN = 18 - \frac{2r}{\sqrt{3}} \quad (2)$$

Equating (1) and (2), we get

$$\frac{4r^2}{3} - 24r + 144 = 324 - 24r\sqrt{3} + \frac{4r^2}{3}.$$

Thus,

$$180 = r(24\sqrt{3} - 24) \;\Rightarrow\; r = \frac{15\sqrt{3} + 15}{4}.$$

Consequently,

$$OD = \frac{2r}{\sqrt{3}} = \frac{15 + 5\sqrt{3}}{2}.$$

Therefore, the radius is

$$QD = OD + r = \frac{45 + 25\sqrt{3}}{4}.$$

25. How many positive integers less than 200 are divisible by the number of its positive divisors?

(A) 19   (B) 20   (C) 22   (D) 24   (E) 25

Answer (E): First note that 1 works. For $1 < n < 200$, n can have at most 3 distinct prime factors, otherwise it would be at least $2 \times 3 \times 5 \times 7 = 210$. We will do casework based on whether the number of prime factors of n is 1, 2, or 3. Let $d(n)$ be the number of positive divisors of n.

- **Case 1:** $n = p^a$
  $d(n) = a + 1$ must divide p^a. Since 2 is the smallest prime number and $2^8 = 256$, this means that $a < 8$. By investigating the possible values of a, we find the following solutions for (a, p): (1, 2), (2, 3), (3, 2), (7, 2). So there are 4 solutions in case 1.

- **Case 2:** $n = p^a q^b$. We'll consider two subcases: $p = 2$ and $p > 2$.
  - **Subcase 1:** $p = 2$, $q \geq 3$. Because $200 > n = 2^a \cdot 3^b \geq 2 \cdot 3^b$, we know that $b \leq 4$

        * $b = 1$
          $a = 2$, $q = 3$
          $a = 3$, $q = 3$, 5, 7, 11, 13, 17, 19, 23
          $a = 4$, $q = 5$
          $a = 5$, $q = 3$

        * $b = 2$ In this case $q = 3$. Then $a = 1$, 2, 3
        * $b = 3$ In this case $q \leq 5$. There is no solution for $q = 5$. For $q = 3$, $a = 2$.
        * $b = 4$ In this case q must be 3. However, there is no solution for $q = 3$.

      So there are 15 solutions in subcase 1.

    – **Subcase 2:** $p > 2$

      This means n is an odd number. So, $a + 1, b + 1$ have to be odd numbers, which means $a, b \geq 2$. Hence, $n = p^a q^b \geq 3^2 \cdot 5^2 > 200$. No solution.

- **Case 3:** $n = p^a q^b r^c$
  If $p > 2$, with similar arguments in Subcase 2, there is no solution. So, $p = 2$. Since, $q^b r^c$ is at least 15, $a \leq 3$

    – $a = 1$
      $2(b + 1)(c + 1) | 2q^b r^c \implies (b + 1)(c + 1) | q^b r^c$. There is no solution according to Subcase 2.

    – $a = 2$
      Then $q = 3$. In this case $r^c < 200/(4 \times 3) < 17$. Since r is at least 5, $c = 1$.
      For $b = 1$, $r = 5$, 7, 11, 13
      For $b - 2$, $r - 5$
      For $b > 2$, $n > 210$.

    – $a = 3$ $q^b r^c < 200/8 = 25$. The only solution to this inequality for $r > q > 2$ is $q = 3$, $r = 5$, $b = c = 1$ which doesn't satisfy the condition.

    So there are 5 solutions in Case 3.

In total we have $1 + 4 + 15 + 5 = 25$ solutions.